CCCC STUDIES IN WRITING & RHETORIC

Edited by Joseph Harris, Duke University

The aim of the CCCC Studies in Writing & Rhetoric Series is to influence how we think about language in action and especially how writing gets taught at the college level. The methods of studies vary from the critical to historical to linguistic to ethnographic, and their authors draw on work in various fields that inform composition—including rhetoric, communication, education, discourse analysis, psychology, cultural studies, and literature. Their focuses are similarly diverse—ranging from individual writers and teachers, to work on classrooms and communities and curricula, to analyses of the social, political, and material contexts of writing and its teaching.

SWR was one of the first scholarly book series to focus on the teaching of writing. It was established in 1980 by the Conference on College Composition and Communication (CCCC) in order to promote research in the emerging field of writing studies. As our field has grown, the research sponsored by SWR has continued to articulate the commitment of CCCC to supporting the work of writing teachers as reflective practitioners and intellectuals.

We are eager to identify influential work in writing and rhetoric as it emerges. We thus ask authors to send us project proposals that clearly situate their work in the field and show how they aim to redirect our ongoing conversations about writing and its teaching. Proposals should include an overview of the project, a brief annotated table of contents, and a sample chapter. They should not exceed 10,000 words.

To submit a proposal, please register as an author at www.editorial manager.com/nctebp. Once registered, follow the steps to submit a proposal (be sure to choose SWR Book Proposal from the drop-down list of article submission types).

REDESIGNING COMPOSITION FOR MULTILINGUAL REALITIES

Jay Jordan
University of Utah

Conference on College Composition and Communication

National Council of Teachers of English

Portions of Chapter 1 appeared previously in "Feminist Composition Pedagogies in ESL Tutoring," *Gender and English Language Learners*, ed. Bonny Norton and Aneta Pavlenko (Alexandria: TESOL, 2004, 43–56). Portions of Chapter 2 appeared previously in "Second Language Users and Emerging English Designs," *College Composition and Communication* 61.2 (2009): 381, W310–W329, and in "Dell Hymes, Kenneth Burke's 'Identification,' and the Birth of Sociolinguistics," *Rhetoric Review* 24.3 (2009): 264–79. This material is reprinted here by permission from TESOL, Inc.; NCTE; and Taylor & Francis Ltd, http://www.tandf.co.uk/journals, respectively.

Staff Editor: Bonny Graham
Interior Design: Mary Rohrer
Cover Design: Mary Rohrer and Lynn Weckhorst

NCTE Stock Number: 39660

Publication partially funded by a subvention grant from the Conference on College Composition and Communication of the National Council of Teachers of English.

Library of Congress Cataloging-in-Publication Data
Jordan, Jay, 1973-
  Redesigning composition for multilingual realities / Jay Jordan.
    p. cm. — (CCCC studies in writing & rhetoric)
  Includes bibliographical references and index.
  ISBN 978-0-8141-3966-0 (pbk.)
1. English language—Composition and exercises—Study and teaching (Higher)
—Foreign speakers. 2. English language—Rhetoric—Study and teaching. I. Title.
  PE1404.J66 2012
  808'.0428—dc23
                                                        2012013107

\# 791489820

For Cecil Terrell Jordan and George Allan McLeod.
Whenever I have been unsure, I have tried to imagine what
they would do.

CONTENTS

PREFACE

DOUBTLESS MANY BOOKS START IN some way with Peace Corps service. Mine did. Even though my own service as an English as a second language (ESL) teacher in a teacher training college in Poland was relatively short, it taught me about being a language learner in a place where you have to rely for the most part on your second language for daily life. The only other people in the city my former wife, Stefanie, and I lived in who knew English were fellow teachers, and they didn't moonlight in the grocery store, the market, the train station, the bus station, or the post office. So we resorted to our "survival Polish" whenever we weren't at school or in our apartment. We had great Polish teachers during the three months of training before we settled into our assignment, but that three months wasn't quite enough to bridge the distance between our southern English and Polish, a heavily Slavic tongue. We could order tickets to Warsaw, and we could pick out bread and other essentials in our local store, but we needed our dictionaries, declension tables, and advance planning before we felt confident enough to navigate something like "Could I have a quarter kilo of your best kiełbasa, please?" As often as not, the Poles we spoke to responded to our efforts with amusement, surprise, or annoyance. During the twentieth century, many Poles immigrated to the United States, so it hadn't occurred to the Poles in our town that Americans would come to Poland, even though we were probably the fifth pair of Peace Corps volunteers to live in that town. So most people probably didn't assume we were Polish-as-a-second-language speakers. They just thought we were slow Poles.

I had tacked up in our kitchen numerous charts that showed how to decline several classes of Polish nouns and adjectives. If I got into a sticky grammatical situation over the phone, I could easily take a step or two into the kitchen, find the right chart, track down the right ending, and put it on the word I needed—right about the time the person at the other end of the phone gave up. We knew a lot about Polish grammar, actually—more than our Polish friends. More than the people who worked in the shops along our walk to school. More even than Lech Wałęsa, who is infamous among his countryfolk for his ability to botch their beloved language. But we got little if any credit for our language competence. Our friends laughed at my declension charts, albeit good-naturedly. Shopkeepers and bus drivers would often feign misunderstanding about products or names of cities until we pronounced them exactly right. Stefanie said that learning and using Polish was like having a bad boyfriend (or girlfriend): When things went well, you were really, really happy, and you kept coming back. When things went badly, they were horribly, horribly wrong.

I remembered our frustration when we returned to the United States. I won't say that I immediately became more patient with the English language learners who were fast becoming a presence to be reckoned with in North Carolina, our home state. But I recall having flashbacks while I stood in line at a motor vehicles office in Charlotte behind several Spanish speakers trying to get licenses. Some of the facial expressions of the attendant behind the counter looked familiar. I remembered our frustration again when Stefanie and I went to Penn State. Her teaching in the Intensive English Program and in pronunciation courses for the Department of Linguistics and Applied Language Studies put both of us in contact with English language learners from all over. Mostly graduate students, these people were living thousands of miles from spouses and children; were building second careers; were learning to refine English as their third, fourth, or fifth languages. Some were already working for large international companies. A few had their own patents. Whereas Stefanie and I had developed some grammatical competence in Polish, these international students had competencies in English and in other languages I could only guess at. The problem was that they were given relatively few opportunities to display them. Their well-meaning advisors sent them to the writing center and sometimes to basic writing courses. The undergraduates these students taught complained about their accents and even, at times, that they didn't seem to know English at all. Their attempts to cram their experience and knowledge into one language—and a carefully policed one at that—inevitably prompted them to rework, invent, make do.

This book is an attempt not only to honor the courage of these learners—something I wish I'd had more of in Poland—but also to recognize their work in keeping English alive—that is, not as a resource just for themselves but for all English users. Undoubtedly, they do some of their work unawares. In fact, many language teachers would say that all of it is unintentional, if not "error." But I had had enough experience to know that was not the whole story, and I needed a way to start hearing, reading about, and telling the rest of it.

A lot of people have supported me as I've looked for a way to tell this story. I am deeply grateful to my advisers and mentors at Penn State—Keith Gilyard chief among them. I also owe thanks for the dedication, humanity, probity, and wisdom of Cheryl Glenn, Paula Golombek, Elaine Richardson, Rich Doyle, Karen Johnson, and Jack Selzer. Paul Kei Matsuda was among the first people I met at my first Conference on College Composition and Communication (CCCC) meeting, and he has been characteristically generous with time and advice ever since. And I make special note of numerous colleagues—first-rate scholar-teachers in their own right—who worked in cubicles just like mine but who were never boxed in: Susan Bobb, Antonio Ceraso, Mark Longaker, Vorris Nunley, Jeff Pruchnic, Stephen Schneider, Marika Seigel, and Scott Wible.

Since 2006, I have been fortunate beyond telling to be part of an incredible group of peers in Utah, including Jenny Andrus, Casey Boyle, Tom Huckin, Maureen Mathison, Susan Miller, and Natalie Stillman-Webb. And I have benefited from the support of Stuart Culver and Vince Pecora, who in their capacity as successive department chairs have consistently advocated for me as I have sought release time and funding. I acknowledge the substantial support of the University of Utah's Department of English, University Writing Program, and College of Humanities.

As this project was completing its evolution into an actual book, Joe Harris, Bruce Horner, and Morris Young generously, astutely, and patiently guided it and me via email, phone conversations, and face-to-face meetings in hurried conference corridors. And Kurt Austin and other NCTE staff did their peerless production work with characteristic efficiency and calm.

I must also recognize the teachers and students of composition who have allowed me to watch, listen to, record, and write about their important work. I cannot name them here, but I hope I have honored their efforts. There is no way for a researcher not to impose her or his own agenda on a work like this, but with their help, I have sought a balance.

And last and most important, my family and closest friends. Phyllis and Terry Jordan have called me "Professor" for as long as I can recall, and they were confused when I decided to go to law school. They were relieved when I left, and they were thrilled when I finished a PhD and got a job with it. They continue to support me with calls, letters, visits, and prayers. They have shared that work in recent years with Davis Jordan and Stefanie Rehn. Stefanie and I no longer have a relationship "on paper," but there's no way I could imagine *not* knowing her. And there's no way I could thank her enough for Davis, the son we share, who reminds me to look to the future every day.

REDESIGNING COMPOSITION FOR MULTILINGUAL REALITIES

Introduction: Coming to Terms with "English" "Users" in "Composition"

> Polish was my first language, but English is my first language.
> —Student in ENGL 015, Section 64, Penn
> State University, Fall Semester 2004

> If not "student," what term defines a more desirable situation?
> —Vivian Cook

THIS BOOK IS NOT JUST FOR TEACHERS of multilingual students. Rather, it assumes that multilingualism is a daily reality for *all* students—all language users—whether they themselves use more than one language or whether they interact with others in settings of multiple language contact. Doubtless, some teachers will believe they and/or their students fall into neither category: more than one teacher has told me that the sea of phenotypically similar faces greeting them when they enter their writing classrooms is clear evidence that linguistic diversity happens somewhere else.

In fact, it happens everywhere—even (especially) where English is spoken. In his 2006 Braddock Award–winning article, Suresh Canagarajah, himself no stranger to the movements of English within and across national borders, notes that the spread of English is by no means unidirectional. While it is true that the privileged varieties of the United States, United Kingdom, Australia, Canada, and New Zealand have had significant impacts on global English-language teaching, media, and other cultural phenomena, less-privileged and more apparently "local" varieties have increasing global purchase:

Often it is CNN that carries the diverse Englishes of report-ers, politicians, and informants—not to mention musicians and film stars—into the houses of the most reclusive middle class families in the West. Furthermore, diaspora communi-ties have brought their Englishes physically to the neighbor-hoods and doorsteps of American families. If they are not working with multilingual people in their offices or study-ing with them in schools, Anglo Americans are exposed to WE [World Englishes] in other ways. The new work order involves an international network of production, marketing, and business relationships. . . . At its most intense, the Inter-net presents a forum where varieties of English mingle freely. ("Place" 590)

And, of course, the composition classroom is on this list as well. Po-sitioned as it often is at the entry point to tertiary education across the United States, composition enrolls hundreds of thousands of students who bring with them the effects of the complex evolution of English that Canagarajah details. While my Polish American student quoted in the chapter-opening epigraph perhaps most suc-cinctly summarizes what it means to encounter multilingualism in homes, schools, and workplaces, his statement presents a problem with many of the terms some English users deploy to describe it. Calling some English users *first language* or *native* and calling oth-ers *second language* cannot account for this student's experience: as he demonstrated to me in the assignment that contained this sen-tence and in other ways during the semester he spent in my course, he was aware both of his high level of English competence and of his ongoing immersion in a multilingual family of immigrants for whom Polish still held considerable power.

For at least forty years, the field of composition has wrestled with the impact of multilingualism, and owing to cross-influences of applied linguistics, second language writing, and sociolinguis-tics—perhaps most visible in the "Students' Right to Their Own Language" resolution (Conference on College Composition and Communication [CCCC]) and its subsequent revisions—it has developed ways to theorize this impact. Especially in recent years, scholars at the intersections of the several fields have called attention to gaps between knowledge about multilingualism and practices that would put that knowledge to work in writing instruction. In 1999, Paul Kei Matsuda pointed to a mismatch between multilingual students' movements through composition courses and the institutional and disciplinary boundaries that had solidified between putatively "first" and "second" language writing teaching and research ("Composition"). In ensuing years, relevant conversations across disciplines have increased, as evinced by well-attended interest sections, panels, and workshops at major conferences (especially Teachers of English to Speakers of Other Languages [TESOL] and CCCC) and by collaborative publications (see, for example, Bean et al.; Matsuda, Cox, Jordan, and Ortmeier-Hooper). These conversations have recently prompted the production of a collaboratively written statement in *College English* (signed on to by, at press time, fifty additional scholars) calling for broadly "translingual" approaches to writing instruction—a statement backed by a list of references that would look just as comfortable in the pages of an applied linguistics journal (Horner, Lu, Royster, and Trimbur).

But the important moment of multilingual awareness in composition that this statement represents does not obscure the uncertainty about *how* to make composition more multi- or even translingual. Composition instructors often read scholarly articles with a view toward Monday morning, when students and instructors file back into classrooms to write, revise, and respond. The questions that Horner and his colleagues anticipate ("Does translingualism mean there's no such thing as error?," "Where can I go for help?") are common and understandable ones. Canagarajah concludes his essay on pluralization in composition by admitting his own uncertainty: "I must confess," he says, "that I am myself unsure how to practice what I preach. Throughout my life, I have been so disciplined about censoring even the slightest traces of Sri Lankan English in my own academic writing that it is difficult to bring them into the text now" ("Place" 613). While more and more scholars and teachers of writing are demonstrating a willingness to question assumptions about language—and the role of English in particular

—we also realize that those questions lead to practical problems ranging from the disciplinary locations of writing all the way to how to read a sentence in a student's draft that shows the presence of Polish or Tamil.

This book, then, represents an attempt to bridge where we have been as scholars and teachers of writing in (inevitably and increasingly) multilingual settings to where we are now to what we could be doing to reorient composition as a field and a set of practices. It represents an attempt to take seriously the charges to advance cross-disciplinary understandings of multilingualism and to develop specific pedagogical approaches to it—both of which charges point to a need to, as the title suggests, "redesign" composition. The book draws from applied linguistics, literacy studies, foreign language teaching, rhetoric, second language acquisition, and, of course, composition past and present to attend to what multilingual students and their monolingual peers and teachers are doing and can do. It does not provide a list of pedagogical prescriptions, but it is instead intended to encourage teachers to think and rethink their approaches from their classrooms' and institutions' multilingual realities outward.

ORIENTING TO MULTILINGUALISM IN COMPOSITION

Of all the growing data about English as a second language (ESL) students in the United States, perhaps the most striking "fact" is that no one has a clear idea about how many there are. Because student visas are easy to count, statistics for international students are often cited, and they suggest that more than 670,000 international students were studying in US colleges and universities during the 2008–09 school year (Institute of International Education). But not all international students are ESL students, and many US citizens and permanent residents are ESL users (Harklau, Losey, and Siegal; Roberge, Siegal, and Harklau). This statistical uncertainty translates into a practical uncertainty about who ESL students are, where they are, and how they may best be educated in US contexts.

Regardless of this uncertainty and of the clear institutional divisions that persist between the fields of "mainstream" comp and ESL comp/applied linguistics, there is shared historical confidence in the literature of both fields about what students should be doing, and for whom. Even though both fields are characterized by major differences in teaching philosophies, research methodologies, geographic locations, and political investments, to name a few, the implicit and explicit goals of composition teaching involving ESL students ultimately center on the idea that ESL students should, to the extent that they are able, successfully negotiate entry into English-language communities whose discursive makeup is determined and arbitrated by monolingual native speakers of English.

But this assumption is problematic at best, given the sheer numbers of nonnative English speakers in the United States and abroad—including many areas of substantial US market interest, interaction, and penetration. As Suresh Canagarajah ("Place") and David Crystal have noted, the number of nonnative English speakers surpassed the number of native speakers by the late 1970s, and the non-native-speaking population is expected to represent a supermajority of total English speakers within fifty years. Of course, numbers alone do not translate to authority: the crucial issue for teachers, learners, and all users of language is, as it has always been, the relative power of those who speak and write certain varieties instead of others.

It is no accident that the teaching of writing in the United States gained a secure foothold during the post–American Revolution period of national consolidation and that college-level writing became a nearly universal requirement within a few years after the Civil War. As authoritative histories of composition teaching tell us (see, for example, Berlin, *Rhetoric*, *Writing*; Connors; Crowley; Murphy), both times were marked by a felt need to distribute literacy and other skills necessary to build the American economy while at the same time preserving class distinctions among a growing population by means of enshrining privileged varieties of English. And much of the subsequent history of composition teaching has sustained this dual purpose of preparing as many as possible for entry-level literacy while standing guard at the gate of more belletristic or otherwise fashionable language use. The teaching of writing to

ESL students has arisen from a more overtly pragmatic tradition based on second language writing's direct inheritance from applied linguistics, inheritor in turn of structuralist assumptions about the nature of language use that assume face-to-face communication among equally "competent" speakers of a shared language (Blanton; Matsuda, "Second Language"; Pennycook, "Disinventing," "Myth"; Pratt). Such a premise, which has existed in ESL composition teaching up to the present in many curricula, has located writing in a causally connected skill set, in which the supposedly passive activities of listening and reading necessarily precede speaking, which necessarily precedes writing. Writing, standing at the end of this skill set, was supposed to represent a culmination activity in which language learners of supposedly now native or near-native fluency and accuracy would represent and record their proficiency on the page, demonstrating the ability to convey a message as clearly as possible for their native-speaking arbiters.

The problem with both traditions is that neither attempt to issue passports to incoming speakers or writers is defensible or sustainable. Even a little observation reveals that colleges, universities, the business world, and other contexts that ESL students inhabit do not look or sound the way explicit English-only language policies, No Child Left Behind legislation, and many composition textbooks believe they do. Despite renewed calls (especially in the aftermath of the 9/11 attacks and in the wake of massive job losses during the post-2008 economic downturn) for tightening immigration controls and visa requirements and protecting American jobs and values, prevailing logics of global market capitalism are dictating that diversity works well for business. As several commentators have noted (Berlin, *Rhetoric*, *Writing*; Fairclough; Gee, Hull, and Lankshear), the shift from heavily industrial assembly-line production to service economy–oriented "just-in-time" production, coupled with increasingly rapid international communications, means that businesses are looking for more and better ways to connect to potential customers across a wide geographic area.

These shifts mean that speakers and writers of English as a second language are increasingly considered target consumers for expanding goods and services and increasingly viewed as representatives of the kinds of cultural and linguistic differences that marketers want to capture and leverage, even as these speakers and writers are still consistently positioned by educational administrators and teachers as students *only*. This mismatch points to the need to reconceptualize "ESL students" as fully competent English *users* (cf. Cook, "Competence," "Going Beyond"; Lu, "Essay," "Professing") who have much to teach other users of English as the language continues to grow through global uses and modifications. Specifically, for composition as a whole, the growing presence and power of these English users presents an opportunity to question and reorient fieldwide assessments of the relations among diverse English users and how those relations undergird standards by which successful communication is judged.

RECOMPOSING TERMS

Admittedly, there is considerable slippage in the preceding pages of this introduction. In discussing the relationship of multilingual language users to the fields of "mainstream" and second language composition, I referred to them variously as students, speakers, writers, and users. In addition, I frequently conflated the terms *composition* and *writing,* and I sometimes truncated the term *composition* to *comp.* Finally, while I consistently used the label "English" to refer to the language that is used—with varying degrees of proficiency, comfort, and idiosyncratic, idiomatic, and regional divergences—by upwards of 1.5 billion people (Graddol), I do not mean to suggest that that language is anything like stable or easily labeled. In this section, then, I clarify how I see these terms used, suggest how I think they should be used, and point to how their use in connection with other key terms gives this book both its focus and shape.

English

An early twentieth-century pledge, issued by the National Council of Teachers of English, clearly conveys what would appear to most contemporary compositionists an inexcusably facile—not to say outright objectionable—view of the relationship between privileged varieties of English and students of English:

I love the United States of America. I love my country's flag.
I love my country's language. I promise

1. That I will not dishonor my country's speech by leaving off
   the last syllable of words.
2. That I will say a good American "yes" and "no" in place of
   an Indian grunt "un-hum" and "nup-um" or a foreign "ya"
   or "yeah" and "nope."
3. That I will do my best to improve American speech by
   avoiding loud rough tones, by enunciating distinctly, and
   by speaking pleasantly, clearly, and sincerely.
4. That I will learn to articulate correctly as many words as
   possible throughout the year.

(qtd. in Delpit and Dowdy 29)

More than the connections to efficiency that James A. Berlin discusses in his historical work, and more than the privileging of belle-
trism that Elizabethada A. Wright and S. Michael Halloran notice,
this list is an ideological statement about the connection between
English, schooling, and national character. It is allied with a tradition of schooling in the United States that has sought to equate
English-language proficiency—specifically, proficiency in forms of
English standardized by successive waves of policies aimed at con-
solidating a national identity—with good citizenship.

Composition can look to a long history of critiquing this connection. Many criticisms arose out of compelling sociolinguistic
research that burgeoned during the 1960s and early 1970s and that
saw its culmination in the field of composition in the 1974 passage of the "Students' Right to Their Own Language" (SRTOL)
resolution by the Conference on College Composition and Communication (CCCC). The resolution's background document recognized that the various social movements of the previous decade
deserved more attention in educational policymaking (1). Specifically, it called attention to the challenges to language education
posed by the increasing stature and power of traditionally underrepresented groups. In one prescient passage, the authors note that
"today's students will be tomorrow's employers. . . . English teachers

who feel they are bound to accommodate the linguistic prejudices of current employers perpetuate a system that is unfair to both students who have job skills and to the employers who need them" (14). Against the background of increasing cultural and linguistic uncertainty that the SRTOL acknowledges, the authors propose numerous pedagogical directions for those English teachers, many of whom (if they read it—see Richardson 14) would have no doubt felt unmoored by the argument that teaching a particular standard made less and less sense and that the handbooks they relied on (and still do to a large extent, if publishers are any barometer) were rapidly obsolescing.

In short, then, SRTOL is a document that reflects an infusion of nonprescriptivist sociolinguistic thinking about the relationships English language dialects have with one another and the relationships their different speakers *should* have with the dialects they use. By taking the position that students' dialects acquired before their schooling are systematic, and that they provide students and their teachers with firm bases for language teaching, SRTOL marks the emergence in composition of what Keith Gilyard has termed *bidialectalist* thinking about language variety in colleges and universities (*Let's Flip* 70). On the one hand, such thinking indicates a clear break from conceptions of students' language as deficient and from conceptions of colleges and universities as proving grounds established in part to eradicate differences in language and culture. While this mode of thinking persists in the popular work of, for instance, William Bennett, Linda Chavez, Dinesh D'Souza, and E. D. Hirsch Jr., many language educators—including many in the field of composition—have consistently argued that such a position is ethically and pragmatically suspect.

On the other hand, the bidialectalist position is itself suspect because of the specific relationship it often envisions between so-called home varieties of English and Edited American English (EAE), as well as the sense of clear division among these varieties it perpetuates. In one section, titled "How Does Dialect Affect Employability?," the SRTOL authors recommend that teachers "stress the difference between the spoken forms of American English and

EAE" (CCCC 14). On its face, this suggestion makes sense given the often wide disparities between spoken and written forms of any language and given the relatively conservative formal nature of writing. But later in the same section, the document advises teachers that they should "begin [their] work in composition with [students with diverse 'home' varieties] by making them feel confident that their writing, in whatever dialect, makes sense and is important to us. . . . Then students will be in a much stronger position to consider the rhetorical choices that lead to statements written in EAE" (14–15). Rather than merely a statement about the "differences" between home (oral) and standardized (written) varieties, this is an *evaluative* statement about the relative value and scope of students' varieties and the Variety (with a capital *V*) that is welcome at work and in other public settings. In this view, English-language instruction, while shedding many overt judgments about "deficiency" and the superior quality of EAE, retains the teleological assumption that EAE is—at the very least, pragmatically speaking—*the* form to be acquired by "different" students.

While the approach to English varieties informed by SRTOL was (and still is) ahead of its time, the goal of bringing nonstandard varieties into English classrooms was intended, as reflected by the SRTOL document's preoccupation with "making [students] feel confident" (CCCC 15), to ease students' transitions into apparently more appropriate language forms. In her later-published 1972 presentation at the TESOL conference, Carol Reed led off by assuring her audience that the Brooklyn College students enrolled in an experimental Standard English as a second dialect course were receiving instruction in "Standard English writing skills" within the regular English composition framework (289). Helping students become more comfortable with academic analysis of their home varieties was necessary, Reed argued, to help them understand the sources of their standardized English errors (namely, interference from Black English Vernacular) and assimilate into the academic English community they were, supposedly, "downright eager" to join (292).

Yet the nature of "English" in academies, workplaces, and other communities is now, as it has always been, in flux—a reality that challenges the idea of clear boundaries between "academic," "home," "standard," "second language," and other English varieties. While it is true, as David Crystal reports, that nearly 95 percent of the US population speaks English (118), it is definitely *not* true that all those speak English *natively*. The US Census Bureau indicates that more than 55 million Americans of school age or older speak at least one language other than English at home. Statistics like this one, combined with others that show consistent increases in Latino and Asian population groups, have fueled recurring legislative attempts to establish English as the official language of the United States. Many critics of such legislation, including Crystal, point out that the English-language ship has sailed—that the saturation of English in the United States and in a growing number of countries in what Braj Kachru has called the "outer" and "expanding" circles of global English-language spread indicates that English has, in fact, solidified itself as a large-scale lingua franca.

But whose English it is is becoming an ever more open question. Disruptions between *both* oral and written forms of English among different English speakers have special significance for the interface between monolingual native-speaking students, second language students, and the academic institutions that bring them together. And a growing number of scholars are questioning the relevance of the native English user model in composition. Drawing on Crystal's descriptive work, Sandra McKay lays out a pedagogy based on teaching "English as an international language," which includes a reassessment of written rhetorical competence based on the idea that readers in so-called inner-circle countries (Kachru) need to assume more responsibility for working to understand texts produced by writers in "periphery" areas (McKay 77–78). In fact, Robert E. Land Jr. and Catherine Whitley articulate a belief that nonnative writers of English have much to teach monolingual readers about how to be more "reader responsible" (Hinds). More squarely in the field of composition, Bruce Horner and John Trimbur argue that writing teachers should "develop an internationalist perspective" while asking critical questions about which Englishes they teach and in what service (624). And, most recently, Horner,

Trimbur, Min-Zhan Lu, Jacqueline Jones Royster, and a growing list of researchers and teachers have signed on to a statement calling for "translingual" approaches to writing that explicitly extend the scope and mission of the Students' Right resolution. In their view, contexts for English use are fluidly changing locally, nationally, and globally, and users' ways of acting with and on language should be understood not only as rights but also as resources (Horner, Lu, Royster, and Trimbur).

Users

In spite of years of descriptive linguistic research indicating that even so-called native speakers of languages continue to learn their language as they encounter new "Discourses" (Gee), it would be difficult to find native speakers of English described as "students" of the language beyond primary school in anything but specialized linguistic, literary, or rhetorical study. It is the putatively nonnative speakers who are the students, invited around the world to join the growing English-speaking community but, more often than not, kept at arm's length as novice community members.

However, a view of English that stresses its development as a function of change and not just of spread reveals that more people are learners of English than they realize and that the stakes of learning English are quite high for everyone. Language learning, then, is less a matter of shifting to an appreciably standard variety and more a matter of maintaining skills in the face of language as a living construct. As Vivian Cook notes in one of the epigraphs to this introduction, such a view clearly challenges the traditional theoretical and pedagogical preeminence of the native speaker, and it also challenges the traditional valence of the term *student*. If native speakers cannot hold the kind of power that many language educators and policymakers assume they hold, and if that takes away the benchmark against which "students" are always already held, then what term works better to describe them?

Cook proposes *user*. He outlines what he terms second language speakers' *multicompetence*—abilities connected to those speakers' negotiations between their first and second languages that are not present in the minds of monolingual native speakers. Cook reminds readers that multilingualism is much more common than monolingualism and that maintaining focus on monolinguals is much like attempting "a description of juggling based on a person who can throw one ball in the air and catch it, rather than on a description of a person who can handle two or more balls at the same time" ("Competence" 67). In an essay more specific to pedagogical concerns, he accepts as uncontroversial the argument that the native speaker is and always will be a native speaker by historical fact of birth, or by what Norman Davies has called the "bio-developmental definition" (Cook, "Going Beyond" 186). The problem, though, comes in where language teaching assumes that native proficiency is, in fact, *the* goal for nonnatives. An additional problem is the assumption that nonnative speakers, to the extent that they do not emulate the linguistic competencies of native speakers, are failed language learners. While Cook does not specifically address the implications of teaching "students" to a standard forever out of reach, he does recognize the unclear boundary between "student" and "user." After all, if teaching language learners to a monolingual standard that is at best impractical and at worst unethical must be abandoned, that does not mean that an alternative immediately presents itself. So what is the final state of a second language learner's learning?

As Yuet-Sim D. Chiang and Mary Schmida note, the answer to this question may have as much to do with the learner's motivation as with her or his relative distance from a monolingual standard: thus, *user*, a term that implies not only more agency but also more ability. Cook proposes a notion of competence based on the idea that any language user who uses two or more languages has cognitive faculties "qualitatively different from those of the monolingual native speaker" ("Going Beyond" 191). While it would be a stretch to characterize Cook's argument as making the claim that second language users have *stronger* language faculties than do monolingual speakers, it is fair to claim some advantages. For instance, Cook notes psycholinguistic experiments that indicate second language users can detect sentences that are rendered in translation with more accuracy than monolinguals can. In addition, bilingual children are more sensitive to grammatical properties of their first languages than many monolinguals are. And, of course, second language users are apt to code-switch—a particularly effective intercultural rhetorical strategy unavailable in the same way to monolinguals.

Ultimately, however, Cook's "user" is still a "speaker," which makes sense for a large number of second language and foreign language courses,[1] in which speaking is the predominant activity. Min-Zhan Lu provides a connection to composition. While Lu does not reference Cook, she does invoke the language "user" as a figure who deploys linguistic choices deliberatively—that is, a figure who considers her or his choices in the light not only of past standardization and tradition but also, crucially, of future opportunities:

> I have in mind the work students perform in both reproducing and reshaping standardized rules of language in the process of using them; retooling the tools one is given to achieve one's ends; and more specifically, retooling the tools according to not only one's sense of what the world is but also what the world ought to be. ("Composition's" 193)

Introducing *ought* into such a perspective on what diverse language users do is an explicit response to more traditional views of what language ought to be and of what students should learn about language. Rather than students' replicating (via whatever pedagogy) accepted forms that can be easily recorded in handbooks, Lu has in mind a richer depiction of language drawn from her reading of Toni Morrison's 1993 Nobel acceptance speech. In that address, Morrison rejects censored language as dead and embraces as alive language that "limn[s] the actual, imagined, and possible lives of its speakers, readers, and writers" (qtd. in Lu, "Essay" 20). Here is a view of symbolic production at once multimodal and forward-thinking—one that cannot help but anticipate how English is spreading *and changing*.

The shift from *student* (especially *ESL student*) to *user*, then, is one that foregrounds uncertainties in the future of the spread of

English as it changes and is changed by diverse local conditions. It also foregrounds the role that *all* users—whether teachers or students, center or periphery—have in deploying their own, deliberative uses of language. As I discuss in later chapters, this shift has specific ramifications within and beyond traditional composition courses, where these different users and their often divergent uses intersect, often with very high stakes.

Composition

Diverse English users interact frequently in many settings, of course, but the composition course as a "gatekeeper" to further study in nearly all disciplines, as well as its location at the point of entry into the intellectual and social environments of colleges and universities, brings such interactions and their outcomes into relief. In the context of adult (returning) students in the United Kingdom, Roz Ivanič has argued for the importance of studying "crucial moments in discourse" that occur at such interfaces:

> [These students] have not had a smooth, uninterrupted path through the education system like regular undergraduates, so what is demanded of them is unlikely to "come naturally." Returning to study represents a turning-point in their lives, when other adult commitments and experiences—other social worlds—are juxtaposed with the academic world. In such circumstances, they are caught up in conflicting social pressures when writing. Whatever aspect of writing we are interested in is therefore likely to be thrown into sharp focus by studying these writers. (5–6)

In fact, *all* students experience jangling juxtapositions of academic and social worlds, with nonnative users of English often feeling them most keenly as they negotiate familial, cultural, and academic demands, often in at least two languages. So while I question the dichotomy Ivanič establishes here, I agree that studying students at this interface can clarify the points at which what "comes naturally" for them meshes (or not) with what is being asked of them, as well as clarify moments in which what students already know should be more valued.

As overall enrollment in US colleges and universities in the early twentieth century increased, second language (L2) users also began attending in increasing numbers alongside their native-English-speaking peers.[2] And since composition had become a required course at many colleges and universities by this time, increasing enrollment overall of second language speakers meant more second language students in composition. As teachers and administrators took notice, they began to explore what the presence of those students meant. The 1950s saw a surge of interest at the CCCC Annual Convention in second language writing issues, but this "mainstream" interest began to taper as the field of L2 composition began to emerge with scholar-teachers who were interested in pursuing their own paths to professionalization—largely through venues like the University of Michigan's English Language Institute that existed outside the purview of CCCC. This separate professional development led to the mid-1960s establishment of Teachers of English to Speakers of Other Languages as a separate conference and, more broadly, to what Paul Kei Matsuda has called the "disciplinary division of labor" in composition studies, which has seen the evolution of separate pedagogical and research traditions, literatures, and departments devoted to mainstream and to L2 composition ("Composition").

Initial efforts to create second language writing pedagogies borrowed heavily from structuralist and behaviorist assumptions about language learning—namely, that writing was basically recorded speech and was thus teachable via methods designed for speaking, and that writing was best taught through a series of carefully controlled practice sessions. As Linda Lonon Blanton observes in her personal history of development as an L2 writing teacher, most of her colleagues throughout the 1960s and 1970s believed that language learning effectively started over in a second language, which meant that language learners needed to begin at the beginning—with listening and speaking, not reading and writing. There was, Blanton observes, no sense of transfer of literacy skills. This view would be challenged most directly and (in)famously by linguist Robert Kaplan. Kaplan, heavily influenced by both Francis

Christensen's generative model of paragraph writing and the Sapir-Whorf hypothesis that tied specific linguistic practices to specific cultures, argued that paragraph structures reflected student writers' first cultural and language influences. The field of contrastive rhetoric, which developed largely on the basis of Kaplan's work, has attempted to articulate textually based differences in the writing of first language and second language students in the forty years since Kaplan's study was published (Connor, "Changing," *Contrastive*, "New Directions"; Kaplan, "Contrastive," "Cultural," "What"; Kubota; Kubota and Lehner; Leki, "Cross-Talk"; Matsuda, "Contrastive"; Panetta).

Alongside the growth of contrastive rhetoric as an explanation for second language students' compositions, other approaches have developed that reflect L2 composition scholars' and teachers' complex relationship with mainstream composition studies. While L2 composition and applied linguistics continue to focus more on textual features of students' writing than mainstream composition does, it has nonetheless also been influenced by the growth of the process approach. Vivian Zamel is credited with introducing process-oriented thinking to the L2 context: she argued in a 1976 essay that second language writers were not as different from native-English-speaking writers as many teachers believed, and so they could stand to benefit from similar approaches. While responses to the introduction of the process approach in L2 composition have varied, many scholars have come to question direct applications of mainstream process-related pedagogies because of their concerns about significant differences among L2 students that, they believe, necessitate more directive writing pedagogies (see Silva). More forcefully, however, teachers invested in the idea that writing classrooms should prepare students to enter academic and professional communities have argued that process approaches are impractical, if not unethical (Horowitz; also see Johns, *Text*; Johns and Dudley-Evans). These advocates of "English for academic purposes" (EAP) have, in turn, been criticized for relying on a pragmatism that allegedly puts them in service of supposedly more established academic disciplines and supposedly fixed professional discourse communities (Benesch; Canagarajah, "Negotiating"; Pennycook, "Vulgar"). For these critics, EAP's strong pragmatic bent begs the question for whom/for what students are writing. EAP practitioners have fired back that considerations of ideology crowd out other important topics and practices in classrooms that, after all, should be about *writing* (see Johns, "Too Much"). Dana Ferris and John S. Hedgcock, in their widely circulating guide, *Teaching ESL Composition*, are explicit in stating that the goal of the second language writing teacher should be to organize student discourse in accord with established generic conventions, using the presence of native-English-speaking students if necessary and if available in order to bring L2 students into fully literate English-using communities.

Given EAP's often intense focus on preparing students to enter academic and professional communities, advocates of more process-oriented, student-centered, discovery-based writing pedagogies appear to stand in sharp contrast. Joan Carson has noted the different evolutions of second language acquisition (SLA) research and of second language composition. She observes that SLA—especially since the development of communicative language teaching approaches—has primarily diachronic concerns, whereas L2 composition (and language teaching generally) has primarily focused on synchronic relationships between writers, readers, texts, and rhetorical or other exigencies for writing in particular situations (also see Raimes). "Writing to learn" may be seen as a corrective to this focus, which accounts for Raimes's definition of error as "windows into the mind" or evidence of language development rather than immediate nonconformance with standards or discursive requirements. Teachers abiding by such developmental approaches respond—implicitly and explicitly—to EAP and other firmly reader- or genre-centric pedagogies by stressing writing as an evolving process of negotiation in which the writer's abilities and needs must be taken seriously.

However, many of the assumptions that underlie this approach seem quite similar to those underlying EAP and other pedagogies that stress the development of academic writing skills. Much as articulations of bidialectalist pedagogies in mainstream composition stress teachers' need to make writers more comfortable with the ultimate project of learning and using standardized forms, similar articulations for L2 students leave little doubt about what is supposed to be learned by the end of the course. Ann Raimes, in extending her discussion of the developmental implications of "errors," wants to encourage students to write to communicate however they can, but she worries about "fossilization" among students whose errors are not promptly corrected, ignoring the evidence she herself offers of students' errors actually increasing with explicit correction and grammar instruction.

Even if ready characterizations of acceptably academic or standardized English can be offered to students—a claim called into question by professional writers in several fields (see Schroeder, Fox, and Bizzell)—a few scholars are asking whether such language is the most powerful for diverse learners anyway. While they disagree on the role of race in students' selection of "target" languages, Lynn Goldstein and Awad El Karim M. Ibrahim have observed high school situations in which, for social reasons at least, second language students feel compelled to acquire nonprivileged varieties, especially variations of African American and Afro-Canadian English. It is not difficult, given schools' generally conservative view of language, to imagine educational responses to such tendencies. In fact, strong responses have appeared in the United States in the wake of the 1979 *King v. Ann Arbor* case, which mandated recognition of African American schoolchildren's English varieties; in the Oakland School Board's resolution on the use of Ebonics in teaching; and in repeated legislative attempts at state and national levels to limit the scope of bilingual education (Valdés). These latest "crises" connect worries about students' actual or perceived distance from standardized forms with concerns about the substantial demographic shifts that threaten to make monolingual native English speakers the minority—a concern that will continue to position composition as a politically contentious practice.

As I hope to demonstrate, critiques of specific kinds of composition are not reason enough to abolish either the course or the requirement, even though those arguments seem to return again and again (Connors; Crowley; Leki, "Challenge"). As Keith Gilyard has argued about "basic writing" courses,

> If we do not ask if there is a need for required composition but, rather, if there is a need to teach critical language awareness, of which producing text is a central part, whenever we can command sites to do so, I cannot fathom how the radically inclined can answer in the negative. ("Basic," 38)

Composition commands a great number of sites in colleges and universities across the United States. Increasingly, those sites enroll students whose varying experiences with English and with other languages in and outside the country pose serious critical questions about what "English" does and can do. It makes pragmatic sense to ask what role such a course can play as English-language practices continue to evolve. And it makes equally good pragmatic sense to assume that an ambitious project of teaching "critical language awareness" cannot end in traditional composition classrooms. As I will argue, the project entails broadening "composition" to take fuller account of negotiations among partners who may represent very different backgrounds with, uses for, and goals in English.

OVERVIEW

With this beginning terminological work as a basis, I now turn to an outline of successive chapters, which continue my focus on terms and how they limit and potentially open directions for the compositions of English users in the contemporary US college and university. While my focus to this point has been on terms that actually appear in connection with the teaching and theorizing of composition, I explore in upcoming chapters the effects of additional terms that do not necessarily appear but that, I believe, are invoked by the relatively limited deployment of my initial terms. Specifically, I focus on the truncation of the term *composition* to *comp*—a common enough occurrence in literature, teaching, and conversations at conventions and in seminars and hallways where teaching and thinking about teaching happens. I frame successive chapters using other "comps" that multilingual English users frequently encounter in composition. They are taught quite clearly that they will have to demonstrate broad *competence* with particular, powerful varieties of English to succeed in US colleges and universities and in a world increasingly saturated by English; ensure that their readers and listeners can quickly and easily *comprehend* each syllable they express; and *compensate* for perceived "deficiencies" (or, in more progressive terms, "differences") relative to standardized English.

I should state that I do not intend to argue that the term *composition* is etymologically related to these three additional "comp" terms. And I do not claim that scholars and teachers who regularly use the term *comp* consciously intend to invoke these other terms. Rather, I intend for these terms to frame the several passes I make through the current state of composition in an attempt to triangulate the field's position with respect to multilingual English users. I am not interested in attempting an exhaustive study of the profession using mutually exclusive categories to frame my overview; I am interested instead in borrowing the limited perspectives that several relevant terms give me to open a conversation about what role culturally and linguistically diverse students can play—other, that is, than the role of the always-needy always-student.

In Chapter 1, "Compensation: Fixin' What Ain't Broke," I address the term *compensation* and its significance for second language users in the US academy. Once multilingual users pass tests of comprehensibility and enter mainstream composition courses, they are frequently expected to make up the perceived "difference" or "deficiency" between their performance and that of native-English-speaking students. This compensatory work is usually outsourced to other administrative units that act, in Stephen North's words, as "fix-it shops" to provide short-term solutions when composition instructors are unprepared or uncomfortable addressing apparent deviations from formal norms. Just as the truncated term *comp* serves multiple conceptual duties, "fixing" multilingual users also takes on more sinister conceptual baggage to the extent that these students are "fixed" or interpellated into their institutionally attributed identities as language learners—an act based on a set of assumptions and practices that can overdetermine their relationships with teachers and other students (Ibrahim).

Chapter 2, "Competence: Learning from 'Learners'," turns to empirical research on diverse multilingual English users' symbolic repertoires as they emerged in composition courses at three universities. These repertoires demonstrate kinds of competence that composition and related fields are only recently recognizing as disruptive of traditional notions of competent language use. *Competence* is perhaps the most common, most historically significant, and most problematic term that diverse multilingual English users encounter. This chapter argues that the diverse skills of negotiation that so-called English language learners often demonstrate position them as models of competence for changing symbolic practices rather than the always-different always-students that many designations, such as "ESL," consider them. Leveraging these competencies will require a shift from the identification, isolation, and containment that has characterized "multicultural" curricula to a "viral" model that integrates lived experiences of cultural and linguistic diversity into curricula at large (Gee). I further argue that first-year composition courses are ideal sites to begin such a shift, since they already position students at a liminal moment in their own language and social development (Ivanič).

Chapter 3, "Composition: Outdated Assumptions to New Architectonics," reports on data collected from my observations of interactions between native-English-speaking and non-native-English-speaking students in a piloted "intercultural" composition course. The chapter focuses on the challenges both instructors and students faced as well as the ways students combined the competencies I note in Chapter 2. It is informed by broad definitions of *composition* that draw on Kenneth Burke's notion of composition as an architectonic for an era of material and symbolic uncertainty (*Permanence*), Keith Gilyard's articulation of composition as a site for "critical language awareness" ("Basic Writing"), and the New London Group's and Richard Kern's discussion of composing as "re-designing" based on "available designs."

Chapter 4, "Composing Intercultural Relationships," suggests specific directions for intercultural composition pedagogy, drawing on largely European models of "intercultural communicative competence" in foreign language learning. Although shifting from clear targets for competence to emerging methods for successful intercultural communication poses real challenges for teachers, I argue that foundations already exist for enlarging composition's scope. And I argue that the payoff for all language users—all *composers*—is great.

NOTES

1. Language teachers conventionally distinguish between teaching a "foreign language," or a language that is not widely used in communities just outside the classroom, and teaching a "second language," or a language in which students find themselves immersed even outside the classroom. The distinction is also conventionally synonymous with the difference in the World Englishes paradigm between "outer circle" countries (the United States, United Kingdom, British Commonwealth countries, and former British colonies) and "expanding circle" countries (China, Japan, Germany, and other countries in which English is a lingua franca but not as pervasive as a language of everyday communication).

2. I do not recapitulate here the history of "mainstream" composition since the late nineteenth century. See Berlin, *Rhetoric, Writing*; Brereton; Connors; Crowley; Murphy; Wright and Halloran.

1

Compensation: Fixin' What Ain't Broke

> [T]he inclusion of new members can . . . create a ripple of new
> opportunities for mutual engagement; these new relationships
> can awaken new interests that translate into a renegotiation of
> the enterprise; and the process can produce a whole generation
> of new elements in the repertoire. Because of this combination
> of an open process (the negotiation of meaning) and a tight sys-
> tem of interrelations, a small perturbation somewhere can rap-
> idly have repercussions throughout the system.
>
> —Etienne Wenger

THE IDEA THAT "MAINSTREAM" COMPOSITION classes are homogeneous,
monolingual spaces is mythical and outdated (Matsuda, "Myth").
The increasing presence of multilingual English users disrupts the
tacit narrative that cultural and linguistic diversity is something to
be presented and studied in texts rather than something to be ex-
perienced and negotiated daily (Grobman; Jamieson; Jordan, "Between," "Rereading"). But composition pedagogies have not necessarily kept pace with this trend: where they have been unable to
convert diverse speech and writing into immediately comprehensible forms "at the door," they have often sought to eradicate them
entirely or, more recently, repair them. In both instances, administrators, instructors, commentators, and policymakers have discussed such diversity in what I call "bacterio-logical" terms—terms,
as I will explain, that characterize such diversity as a contagion that
must be located, identified, and contained for the benefit of the
student-carriers themselves, their peers, and the institutions they
enter. While I do not claim that all would-be bacteriologists in this
metaphor are consciously deploying this language in an attempt to

pathologize multilingual students, I do claim that ways of think-ing, talking, and writing about these students have evolved such that it is difficult to find *other* ways to think, talk, or write about them. Many well-meaning composition teachers, that is, describe their students' language use—even when those students use it in response to specific rhetorical exigencies and/or even when it rep-resents possibly productive, novel uses of English—as a problem, because the assumption of difference as deficit is ideological in its pervasiveness. And this assumption persists in the face of cultural, economic, linguistic, and scholarly trends that point to the specific value of difference—not difference as merely interesting or vaguely enriching, but difference as *essential.*

This chapter focuses on the prevalence of *compensation* in com-position's relationship to multilingual English users. I turn to writ-ing centers as a prevalent example—a favorite destination for com-position's "outsourcing" of diverse language practices. But I am also interested in writing centers as sites where possible responses to this outsourcing present themselves. I then take a theoretical turn to chart what I call a "viral" alternative to prevailing bacterio-logics in composition theory and teaching that reflects preferred—if not necessary—cultural and linguistic practices in a variety of endeav-ors. By laying out this theoretical outline, I mean to focus specific attention on the problem of multilingual users' fixed, quarantined status, and I mean to point to the possibilities that their "novice" standing represents for the whole community of English users. I also mean to introduce the theoretical assumptions that I opera-tionalize, affirm, and question in reporting my empirical observa-tions in subsequent chapters.

LIMITED SPACES, LIMITED PRACTICES?

The increasing presence of multilingual users is obviously not a guarantee that teachers and students in composition will compli-cate static ideas about diversity. Certainly, at one level, multilingual users themselves may not want to call attention to their abilities, backgrounds, and differences because of the stigma that the "ESL" label continues to hold (see, e.g., Chiang and Schmida). Furthermore, when they do, the complicating fact of their presence may be co-opted into straightforward narratives that existed before they entered the classroom about who they are, where they are from, and what they are expected to do. In his research on Franco-African English users in a Canadian high school, Awad El Karim M. Ibrahim noticed just such an overdetermined narrative at work. In the high school Ibrahim observed, 70 percent of students were international—the majority of that figure being African. Yet Ibrahim himself, with the exception of a temporary Black guidance counselor, was the only adult of color in the school during his study. Ibrahim noted that the Francophone African students he observed were simultaneously pressured to learn English to interact with their predominately Anglophone peers and teachers and co-opted into Black American identities that reflected an elision of the difference between North American and African experiences. In other words, the African students arrived in their Canadian environment only to occupy "Black" subjectivities that largely White students and teachers had long since carved out for them without knowledge of African experiences. In another study, this one of students shifting from high school L2 courses to college, Linda Harklau noted that teachers at both levels maintain "archetypes of ESOL [English speakers of other languages] students that have the effect of fixing meaning, lending fleeting identities the sense of normalcy, common sense, and timelessness in a particular social setting" (40). In their high school classes, the students in Harklau's study benefited from such archetypes, which cast second language students as committed and hardworking. In college, though, the equation of "ESL" with "international" gave rise to culturally and linguistically inappropriate pedagogies (e.g., writing assignments about "your country") that left students frustrated and unmotivated.

For better or worse, many multilingual users who find themselves in composition courses much like those that Ibrahim and Harklau describe are directed to writing centers, which often serve as spaces to quarantine and/or inoculate students whose language practices diverge from acceptable standards. But despite—or perhaps because of—this position, writing centers can simultaneously be spaces where students' cultural and linguistic differences can be more fully explored than many composition classes allow. For various reasons, it is usually difficult to argue for pedagogical and institutional change from the writing center; however, the changing perspectives multilingual users and their language uses represent present not just ethical but also *pragmatic* imperatives for change, which may give arguments originating from writing center tutors and administrators added weight.

Similar to the development of composition and basic writing throughout the twentieth century, writing centers arose largely in response to growing numbers of students entering colleges and universities—especially students whose cultural and linguistic backgrounds did not initially dispose them to enter academic discourses. Inasmuch as composition courses inherited their status as places of largely preparatory, if not remedial, work from their early history at Harvard and other, similar institutions, writing centers have been even further removed from upper-level academic work. Stephen North has famously observed that writing centers are traditionally "fix-it shops" to which students and faculty members are continually tempted to outsource examples of writing to be worked on and returned—a perception that has garnered writing centers the reputation of housing potentially important but ultimately ancillary work. Neil Lerner tells a somewhat different history of vacillation between periods of "punishment and possibility" in which, at various times, writing centers housed novel and productive experiments and instances of true student–teacher–tutor cooperation.

But even Lerner recognizes that these moments have largely been overshadowed by writing centers' limitations. Feminist scholars have offered a useful way to characterize the dual nature of writing centers' work and reputation: they claim that the teaching of writing has been slow to shed its identification as "women's work," a concept that arose during the industrial era. Susan Ellen Holbrook outlines the characteristics of such work: it is done mostly by women, it is usually service oriented, it pays noticeably and usually substantially less than "men's work," and it is otherwise discursively and materially devalued. In the academy, this gendering of labor translates into the well-known but artificial division between "service" courses—institutionally perceived as "feminine"—and advanced, theoretical courses perceived as predominately "masculine" (202–5). Composition clearly falls into this division on the feminine side, as a nurturing introductory course that coaches beginning students in academic prose, the lingua franca of more rigorous, higher-level work. Janet Bean argues that writing centers share composition's feminized status (128). But if composition—not only as a discipline but also as an administrative unit—is feminized, writing centers appear doubly so. They often have to beg for funding not from "the provost," as Bean suggests, but from English departments and composition programs themselves (127). Not only is the physical space of the writing center limited, but so are perceptions of the work done there—even perceptions of those who work close to them. Elizabeth Boquet recounts, for instance, her confrontation with a senior faculty member who complained about noise from the writing center that, for Boquet, represented interesting and varied work among student tutors and their supervisors. The professor complained that "parties" were not appropriate for the center, given its location in the main faculty building, and that the presence of the noise represented disrespect for the more important and appropriate work he was doing (xiii–xiv).

Such attempts to contain both the "noise" and the work of composition and writing centers mirror traditional attempts to package what many administrators, teachers, and students no doubt consider the "noise" of multiculturalism. But just as static multicultural pedagogies gloss over the complexities of multicultural interactions, the location of composition and the work of writing centers in avowedly service roles mask complexities that may make the field a more productive one because of its marginalized role. I see a striking parallel, for instance, between the space of the writing center and the spaces Cheris Kramarae attempts to carve out for women to "find ways to talk 'out of order'" in "bathrooms and hallways of offices" and "in the lunch areas of factories" (qtd. in Foss, Foss, and Griffin 48). In these borrowed and liminal spaces—outside of and in between spaces of masculinized power—Kramarae believes "women's world" can be constructed as a healthy alternative to men's world. Similarly, where North sees the sometimes sparse furnishings of the writing center as an unquestioned limitation, Marie Wilson Nelson finds that multilingual English users in her pilot group writing program comfortably used the "ragged old overstuffed chair that [a] tutor found for $5 at Goodwill" (30). Whatever the furniture looks like in any given writing center, the space of the center itself is self-consciously not a classroom: small tables replace desks and podiums, bookcases and eclectic selections of readers and handbooks replace required texts, and conversation replaces evaluation. Second language users who enter the writing center are often acutely aware of this difference. Their sensitivity is not surprising given their frequent exposure in L2 writing classrooms to teaching based on mechanical correctness and direct grammar instruction. In her survey of multilingual users seeking writing center tutoring, Muriel Harris found that, despite prevailing conceptions in mainstream and second language composition studies that multilingual students come to the writing center looking for another opportunity to be told "what to do," they overwhelmingly expect sessions that open with "friendly conversation" and that proceed on the basis of "advice" (223, 227). My own, more limited, survey in one writing center revealed that at least some multilingual users perceive open-ended sessions to be more productive than classroom interactions: one responded that "even thought I make a big big mistake, I will willing to change it after I talk to my tutor. But with my teacher, I will feel that I am forced by my teacher to change."[1]

However multilingual English users like their tutoring sessions to proceed, there is considerable agreement among tutors and administrators that the best sessions are those that work through errors as efficiently as possible, usually following a more directive approach than most tutors (and, in many instances, students) are initially comfortable with. Commentators often paint a picture of hurried sessions with students and their tutors perched over drafts, while a line of other students waits just outside the room. In such a situation, probably replicated at many writing centers, especially where first-year composition courses (and their deadlines for assignments)

are more or less standardized, "advice" can quickly become training. One student tutor, feeling just such time pressure, would trun-
cate a potential discussion about a second language user's "error":

> For example, an ESL student might write this sentence: "My
> sister suffers by leukemia." The sentence should read: "My
> sentence suffers *from* leukemia." With many other pages to
> read and other students waiting to be tutored, my best expla-
> nation is this: "We just don't write it that way." (Wills 9)

Time in writing centers is often at a premium, so working through
this user's apparent idiomatic confusion would require time that
may not be available. In composition classrooms, teachers who
agree that multilingual users have much to teach might feel em-
powered to revise their class schedules the way bell hooks would
suggest—purposefully slowing down circulations of texts and comments in order to find possibilities other than mastery. However,
the constraints of the writing center mean that tutors and administrators often feel no such authority.

The ultimate limits on general writing center pedagogies combine with typical responses to multilingual users to enforce ideas of
efficiency even further—even where tutors claim to be expanding
students' options for critical participation. Much like the figure of
the recalcitrant native English reader that emerges in L2 composition pedagogy, the figure of the demanding teacher controls multilingual user–tutor interactions in many writing center settings.
In a reflection of the "ethic of care" that Aaron Schutz and Anne
Ruggles Gere note in service-learning courses, the writing tutor often embraces a sense of the need to save students from their own
errors and from the harsh evaluations of their faculty and peer readers. Here, then, the tutor's best intentions and her or his position
in relatively powerless writing centers unite to overdetermine the
possible roles that multilingual users can play. So, as much as terms
such as *negotiation* and *revision* circulate in tutors' accounts of their
work, the agentive possibilities these terms can open for students
are necessarily limited by a sense of time constraints and by the
tutors' sense of what will most help their multilingual clients. The

OED defines *negotiation* in several ways, all of which imply more or less equal-status interactions.[2] It defines *revision*—in terms probably not surprising to compositionists schooled in process approaches—literally as "re-seeing," and while some of the definitions emphasize re-seeing toward a goal of improvement or correctness, what *those* terms mean is open for deliberation. Both definitions in effect stress what rhetoricians should readily identify as invention, a moment of rhetorical possibility that Mikhail Bakhtin would recognize as an opportunity for a language user to join historical, current, and future utterances. As is clear in the quotation that opens this chapter, learning theorist Etienne Wenger would see both processes as essential to encouraging and leveraging "perturbations" that can have heuristic repercussions in exactly the kinds of communities that compositionists want to prepare students to enter.

However, this meaning is not usually apparent where the two terms crop up. Jessica Williams, for instance, in a landmark issue of the *Journal of Second Language Writing* devoted to L2 users in writing centers, is leery of the embrace of "conversation" as a model for student–tutor interactions because she does not see how to capture the effects of such conversation on measurable written revisions. As Williams uses the term, *revision* clearly comes to refer to conformance with the norms of EAE as applied (often tacitly) by monolingual native English speakers. Initially, Williams posits that revision may be initiated by writers themselves and not necessarily by teachers, peers, or tutors—a realization that might predispose tutors and administrators to look and listen closely for students' agendas (174). Later, though, Williams connects effective "revision" with tutors' use of directive language to ensure that the sentence- and word-level advice they give is quickly comprehensible to multilingual clients for their immediate application in writing (186). Similarly, *negotiation*—a kind of god-term among compositionists of several schools, and especially those interested in helping students enter discourse communities—seems, in this context, one-sided. Williams and Carol Severino, in the same *JSLW* issue, cite several studies to ask the question, "What is the optimal balance between pushing L2 development through *negotiation of form* (i.e., prompting learners to self-correct) and simply providing them with the information they may lack through models or direct instruction of the L2?" (167, emphasis in original). That is, where "negotiation" outside of this context refers to give-and-take between at least potentially equal-status partners, here it refers to a process of accession to correctness that is perhaps somewhat less directive than simply giving the answers.

Although messier and no doubt more time intensive than efficient "negotiations" toward EAE, there are alternatives that seem to encourage not only more active participation from multilingual English users but also more potentially productive language deliberation. Deborah Brandt argues that, while cultural expectations about what constitutes "literacy" do evolve (from strictly print to online media skills, for instance), vestiges of old practices always remain, as do traditional expectations. So, for instance, office managers and proofreaders might continue to insist on handbook accuracy in business documents even when clients who receive and use the documents would rather they conform to more local usage. In this view, continuing insistence on negotiation and revision as processes that inevitably lead to edited correctness in American English may be read as evidence of conflict between traditional and contemporary literacy needs. It is not surprising that such conflict would work itself out in the contemporary writing center, which is at once a place where diverse student writers and language users are most concentrated and a place where resource limitations (and limitations of perspective) mean that writing center workers must respond to long-standing institutional expectations about diverse students. Even though many writing center workers and theorists comment that the combination of diversity and resource limitation inevitably produces conflict, I see the combination as a laboratory of language contact—one that can produce shifting perspectives on language diversity in the (writing) center from a *problem* to be contained and, ultimately, eradicated, to a *resource* to be encouraged and spread.

One way to begin this shift is to encourage a broader sense of negotiation and revision. Instances in writing center literature and in my own observations and interviews as a full-time writing center tutor point to moments in which, in a traditional, bacteriological perspective, things are getting out of hand. Rather than ignore these moments as outliers or attempt to contain and treat the student practices that arise during these moments, I suggest rethinking them in viral terms that, as I will discuss, more closely ally with historical and current movements in and out of the field of composition.

EVIDENCE OF (TRUE) NEGOTIATION: REREADING MULTILINGUAL USER–TUTOR INTERACTIONS

Not everything that happens during writing center tutoring sessions is relevant to the paper or project the student client is working on. In fact, to many tutors that sentence probably reads as an understatement. In my experience, students bring to the comfortable space of the writing center not only their writing but also their anxieties, their excitement, their boredom, and their other assignments. I never satisfactorily settled the question of whether to help students with work that wasn't related to their composition courses, though the circumstances under which I was tutoring did help somewhat: as a full-time tutor, I was effectively "teaching" sections of a for-credit course that complemented the first-year writing curriculum, so I could hold that over students who didn't have drafts of their composition work and/or wanted to do something else. But even when students came prepared, they weren't necessarily focused on the task they had thirty-five minutes a week to discuss with me. Feeling time pressures myself, I was often frustrated when students were much more talkative about what seemed to be extraneous topics or material. Certainly, within a framework that stresses the value of efficient development, these episodes were not only frustrating but also potentially detrimental.

Until, that is, they are read differently. One tutor refers to such moments as "mini cultural dialogues that have touched on everything from environmentalism to the role of culinary traditions in preserving cultural values" (Houp 11). In writing classrooms and writing centers that are increasingly multicultural in both population and curricula, such emergences may be not only inevitable but also quite useful. To the extent that such dialogues bring new information to bear on (supposedly) monocultural assignments or on assignments that treat multiculturalism as a worthily studied but distant phenomenon, they can represent moments in which the student is sharing potentially transformative knowledge.[3] I have noticed that dialogues like these can improve students' confidence noticeably: in what is an unusual turn for them, they are encouraged to share experiences from outside the university, which, as Richard Ohmann argued thirty-five years ago, is used to treating students as if they arrived in the classroom from the ether. More encouragement leads to more sharing and, often, even more confidence. The critical question for compositionists and for writing center workers is what to do with that confidence. One response is to channel it into making the students more effective editors of their work in much the way that some of the language in the background document to the Students' Right to Their Own Language (SRTOL) resolution was geared toward affective considerations of language learning. Another response is to channel it into more agency, which can be unpredictable. Beatrice Mendez Newman, who teaches and tutors in the geographic borderland between Mexico and Texas, notes that, although sometimes "tangential" to the writing assignment at hand, "this talk is what helps students see the writing center as the center that can help them hold onto their academic goals" (59). More specifically, she relates that one student whom she helped develop facility with Microsoft Word became confident enough to confront and negotiate (as a more equal partner) with an instructor. In some cases, tutors might learn from students. Another tutor, working with Chinese students in the sciences, relates how she essentially traded English editing knowledge for information about Chinese linguistic practices. She used the metaphor of a freight train to call attention to how compound sentences are written in English. She then learned more about Chinese compounds from a student who was dissertating about reading levels in Taiwanese textbooks (Carrington).

One wonders how many multilingual user–tutor interactions would read (and turn out) differently if this sense of negotiation and revision were applied more consistently and not ruled out as "out of order" or unproductive of good language practice. Terese Thonus writes about serving so-called Generation 1.5 students in writing centers—students who speak English as an (officially) "second" language but whose long-term experiences in the United States often make them relatively fluent speakers, if not writers. One strategy of particular importance for Thonus is ensuring that such students are included in tutorial conversations, thus taking advantage of their fluency, especially in group settings. What is problematic in her analysis of the interchange she highlights, however, is that the student in question, while included in the conversation, is effectively made to serve a particular linguistic end:

> T: I think that S1 was touching something good. ((to S1)) If that's his [S2's] thesis, what does he need to do with the rest of the paper?
> S1: Should, I don't know.
> T: And if we lose track of that being his thesis, then how do we fix that?
> S1: ((to S2)) Kind of tie it in, in the conclusion?
> T: Yeah, that's definitely one way, and probably something that [um]
> S2: So tie in my thesis into the conclusion?
> S1: Yeah, you should, always. (20–21)

While revisiting the thesis in the conclusion is a common rhetorical strategy, it is not the only strategy for reemphasizing an argument or for getting it back on track, as the tutor implicitly points out. However, the student who is, in this interchange, assisting the tutor in conveying the point, ends the interchange by affirming that this should "always" be done. Thonus lets this foreclosure pass without comment, focusing instead on the benefit of generally engaging the Generation 1.5 student, noting that such inclusion is "critical for the . . . student's integration into the group and subsequent development as a writer" (21). Even in a relatively narrow view of developing students as "correct" writers there would be problems with affirming this student's argument that conclusions should always revisit the thesis. For instance, such a strategy might be inappropriate to the rhetorical situation: if the argument were a brief one and/or a written one, rehearsing the thesis may bore or even insult listeners or readers rather than reorient them. In a view of students as agents drawing on diverse knowledges—of English and other languages—that are usually untapped in composition, both the first student and the tutor might wait for the second student's response before shutting down alternatives. While evidence of the first student's confidence is compelling, it should not overshadow the potentially lost opportunity in either the interchange itself or the scholar's research report.

Two more examples further illustrate the point that historical tendencies to view multilingual users as mere novices can obscure potentially productive contributions. Jessica Williams carefully researches connections between particular writing center interactions and subsequent student draft revisions. In one interaction, a tutor is trying to encourage a student to include in a paper about "the American dream" an introduction that provides a general definition of the concept:

> T: What are some of the things that it said about what the American way of life[—]what the American dream is?
>
> S: The American way of life is include the religion and it's just mix with the American culture.
>
> T: This is . . . this essay here was about the American way of life. Do they discuss their[—]or do they talk about the American dream?
>
> S: It just like the American unity by[—]united by religion not focus on the money—
>
> T: —But do they talk about anything, about the wishes . . . the wants[—]the American dream that Americans would or all Americans on people have in America? Because this is a way of life . . . like , . . ah[—]democracy. I just noticed they talk about democracy, free enterprise . . . but do they talk about the dream that people have? The dream of[—]you know. Having . . . a—

s: —I just see the general life had . . . that the general requirements of the dream. It's just like the circumstances—

t: —Okay.—

. . .

t: Okay. So, one of the main things that I've heard from you discussing those papers is something[—] you've been always using the word better. So, maybe from the American dream we can get some . . . we can get something that would improve us more. The American dream is something that would better us as a person. It seems that that's . . . you're using[—]you know[—]we'll get more money[—] a better education. So, it just seems that the American dream is something that will improve us, right? Do you think so or do you think differently?

s: Um, the American dream, she didn't say include my view in the[—]ah[—]my project.

t: I know but we're just trying to get something general to include in your introduction. I don't want you to say[—] you know[—]I believe this[—]I believe that . . . but what we wanna do is get something, something general into[—]um[—]into your introduction paragraph. How[—]um[—]an American dream basically is the defi . . . there is no real definition of what an[—]of what the American dream is. It's gonna be, like you said . . . some of them was about a better education and some of them defined it as more money or working hard to get more money. So, I'm not saying for you to include your opinion but we can include a general, general, very general definition of what the American dream is and the importance of success is in your introductory paragraph. Just so we can introduce your thesis and then[—]ah . . . the survey and then the research.

s: You mean just to write the general information about the American dream?

T: Right, and that's why I asked you what you can get out of those[—]what were the different views? What were the different types of definitions that people gave the American dream? And then from that we can come up with something very general just to have in your introductory paragraph and then include your thesis. (183–84)

It is important to note that this student, like all five students in Williams's study, is a permanent resident of the United States. So, even though this student speaks English as a "second" language, his education in US high schools and his preponderance of US-educated, English-speaking peers means that he is probably much more familiar with US cultural characteristics than his international peers. Part of the context informing this tutor–student encounter, then, is the assignment itself—a common one in second language writing classrooms that asks for reporting on nebulous ideas like "the American dream" that may either be culturally irrelevant to international students or just as clichéd for permanent residents as for many native-English-speaking US citizens. Of course, numerous constrictions on writing center work would limit this (and any) tutor's ability to open the tutoring session to critiques of the assignment, but what Williams codes as the student's "resistance" to the tutor's advice may have more to do with his perceptions of the assignment than with other reasons, such as the student's lack of understanding. It is also possible that the student's understanding of the assignment's rhetorical context made it unclear why he would need a general introduction. Again, the impetus to "revise" often comes from the teacher rather than the student, a point Williams in fact mentions. Likely, this interaction would not occur absent the teacher's direction or some other institutional requirement or advice. Thus, the tutoring situation reinforces the overdetermined relationship between writer and reader that has always obtained in writing classrooms: the reader is the teacher, which may well cause the student (who knows this) to wonder why he needs to introduce "the American dream" to someone who is making him write about it in the first place.

Another "resistant" student receives advice from his tutor to clarify a pronoun's antecedent, which is advice he does not take. Williams classifies this interchange (and the lack of revision that results from it) as one of the "small number of cases" in which the writer seemed to challenge tutorial suggestions:

> T: OK . . . look at this sentence for a second. "Different men have different characters. Some of them are adults who are mature and responsible[—]like my father, who . . . takes care of my mother and of me until I[—]marry . . ." OK. My elder brother[—]OK[—]my elder brother is another example of what?
>
> S: Oh[—]uh[—]of different man.
>
> T: OK . . . so . . . see how you had to go back there and read it. The reader would have to do the same thing, right? Because by the time we get here, right . . . the reader doesn't remember what he read on the other page.
>
> S: *Maybe* they did. *Maybe* they do.
>
> T: Okaaay. [drawn out] *Maybe* [loud] they do, but—
>
> S: —yeah, but if I just read it uh[—]the[—]not stop. I will remember. But if I stop, like[—]I talk to you[—]*maybe* I can't remember. That's the difference.
>
> T: OK. (187–88, emphasis in original)

There is an important point to be made here about this student's competence as well as about conflicts between the tutor's agenda and the student's. The student is apparently well aware of the potential confusion that can result from too much distance between pronoun and antecedent. In fact, he is aware enough to know that reiterating antecedents is not anything like an absolute rule—the decision to reiterate is a matter of judgment based on reading speed and approximations about short-term memory. For the student, the distance between the antecedent and "the other page" is not too long. It is, however, potentially made too long when his reading is interrupted—by the tutor, for instance! A reading of this interchange that privileges evidence of the student's active, equal-status negotiation would point out that the student's final comment is an implicit critique of the tutoring relationship. The student, that is, recognizes that the tutor's intervention produces the very problem the tutor wants to avoid.

INFECTED DISCOURSES AND
THE VALUE OF THE NOVICE

As Nancy Grimm notes in her avowedly political take on writing centers and postmodern conditions, even the very best-intentioned writing center work is still predicated on the idea of ensuring democratic access to privileged forms of literacy. Of course, access is certainly a laudable goal, but pedagogies tied to access often assume the presence of fixed discourses that are legitimate as well as others that are perceived to be illegitimate. Access pedagogies, that is, tend to replicate the kinds of bright-line distinctions between discourses that they seek to break down. Further, these pedagogies are not in keeping with current trends of thought—often operating somewhat afield from composition and literacy studies—about the way communities perpetuate themselves through language practices. Frequently, even privileged discourse communities are both challenged and prodded to develop by language practices that occur outside of officially sanctioned spaces and that represent novel linguistic and rhetorical work. In this final section of the chapter, I lay out a theoretical orientation sensitive to the value not of diversity for its own sake but of diversity for the sake of ensuring healthy communicative environments. In fact, my argument here centers on the specific productive role of so-called novices. I lay out the stakes of reorienting composition from a bacterio-logical basis regarding linguistic diversity (especially where purported novices are concerned) to a *viral* basis on which otherwise alien, infectious influences are allowed to, in Etienne Wenger's words, create ripples of opportunity throughout conservative systems. I move from thinking close to the field of composition (namely, scholarship related to Mikhail Bakhtin and to the study of "discourse communities") to new literacy studies to community and organizational learning theory. By taking this wide sweep, I hope to demonstrate the consistency of viral thinking and its value for composition studies' relationship to its purported language novices.

In a sense, Bakhtin arrived in composition studies with Charles I. Schuster's 1985 introduction of him as a rhetorical theorist. As an alternative to more romantic notions of the author-stylist's exercise of firm control over her or his own prose, Schuster's Bakhtin sees the author/speaker entering a stream of language that existed long before the author and that will continue long after. To the extent that this stream helps determine the author's course, all of the author's decisions are subject to it—even (especially) the aesthetic ones. For Schuster, the "writing that we most value" is that which is most marked by this kind of complexity, in which words and phrases achieve not only internal cohesion but also connections with other contexts (602). As these contexts inform writing more and more directly, they act as a "genuine rhetorical force," shaping the entire discourse, much as ideas of freedom and equality shape nearly every public comment Martin Luther King Jr., ever made, and much as "terror" shapes the discourse of recent US political administrations (595).

Schuster's call for compositionists and rhetoricians to recognize the implications of Bakhtin's thinking was certainly heeded. Bakhtin was beginning to attract notice in the field at the same time compositionists were articulating the importance of dialogue to writing classrooms and especially to process-oriented approaches to writing, with or without teachers. As Kay Halasek has pointed out, "dialogue" has achieved god-term status in composition and has often been so pervasive that it has gone without explicit definition. Much like other terms I interrogate, *dialogue* circulates so widely and is such a comfortable term that it demands scrutiny. As I read Bakhtin's articulation of language's saturation with dialogue, my own scrutiny points to the novice and the novice's influence as a key to the development of language.

Far from describing a simple conversation between speakers, "dialogue" for Bakhtin describes the enduring condition of all language use—even if it appears not to be conversational at all. Bakhtin refers to the mixture of different voices, different contexts, and even different languages in each word as *heteroglossia*, which necessitates a "dialogic" view of how language shapes experience and knowledge. If language is never separable from its context, style is never separable from substance and speaking and writing are never purely originary. Instead, what we as speakers, writers, listeners, and readers must do is constantly attend to the forces that shape language—both as constraints and as possible resources. All language users must deal with constraints on their use, whether imposed by "family, friends, acquaintances, and comrades" (88–89) or by official discourses that demand adherence to local standards. At the same time, all language users may innovate, following the lead of "internally persuasive" rather than "authoritative" discourses. Such innovation inevitably arises from a user's complex interactions with many other language users, who in turn are drawing on internal and external voices in an ever-widening circle. What emerges from this perpetual dialogue is the figure of interlocutors as always-responsive, always-opportunistic potential users of others' words. In fact, Bakhtin sees the role of the Other as essential, and the basic reason why his theory is different from then-dominant linguistic theories that sought to abstract communication from thought.[4] In the terms I am laying out, Bakhtin's view is one of speakers infecting listeners, who themselves become carriers and potential transmitters—hosts for both internally persuasive and authoritative discourse.[5]

It is not difficult to see the specific role diversity and innovation can play, especially when Bakhtin's suspicion of authoritative discourse is accounted for. For Bakhtin, as for several contemporary applied linguists and compositionists (Bawarshi; Bazerman and Prior; Swales, *Genre, Research*), patterns of language use accrue in "genres," which represent more or less stable formal language patterns. If creativity and innovation are, ultimately for Bakhtin, functions of the breadth of a given speaker's generic repertoires, then it is important for that speaker to be exposed to a diversity of speech. Bakhtin is silent about what this diversity might look like. In fact, unlike sketches of *langue* in Saussure or system in Chomsky, predicting the sources of language use in a Bakhtinian perspective is impossible. However, in enlisting Bakhtin in helping her point to a "pedagogy of possibility" for composition, Kay Halasek at least provides a preferred source. She notes that the critical pedagogies of Paulo Freire and bell hooks insist on "integrating" students into official discourses rather than assimilating them. On cultural and linguistic levels, this means encouraging students to "interanimate" their words with more dominant ones, thus slowly changing discourses as they are in turn changed by them. Both Freire and hooks are invested in empowering underrepresented students by valuing their pre–classroom experiences and skills, and Halasek is explicit about what this should mean for composition. Rather than always telling students what they must do as junior members of the academy, teachers must recognize that students who have already negotiated (in the full meaning of that word) numerous discourses before entering classrooms are hosts of internally persuasive discourses that they should be encouraged to cultivate and spread.

Beyond Bakhtin's influence in composition, new literacy studies also point to the value of diverse substrates for productive language infections. I follow here the work of James Paul Gee; Brian Street; David Barton, Mary Hamilton, and Roz Ivanič; and others who view the teaching and learning of literacy not as initiation into "reading" generally or as a clear break from illiteracy or orality, but rather as contextually grounded abilities to engage and negotiate discourses, whether oral, written, or mixed. Both Gee and Street propose a focus on literacies that studies of schooling miss. In the course of building alternative definitions, both theorists suggest that literacy is—regardless of context—a mixture of reading and enacting. Literacies, for Gee, are ways of working in and through what he terms *Discourses* (with a capital *D*), which are "ways of being in the world, or forms of life which integrate words, acts, values, beliefs, attitudes, and social identities, as well as gestures, glances, body positions, and clothes, [producing] opportunities for people to be and recognize certain kinds of people" (127). Two elements of Gee's thinking are especially relevant here. First, literacy, as Gee argues, involves "mastery" of Discourses, which in turn involves abilities beyond the skill of reading and producing print or other representations of language alone. Specifically, Gee's listing of paralinguistic and nonlinguistic features such as gesture and physical appearance suggests real-time, spontaneous interaction. Such a broad definition of literacy implicitly questions the value of evaluation based solely on a unidirectional writer–reader relationship. In fact, Gee goes on to argue that varied experiences with diverse Discourses is necessary if students are to develop cognitive "meta-awareness" (140). Second, the connection Gee makes between using Discourses and "doing *being*" (124, emphasis in original) lays the groundwork for Gee's explicit and Street's more implicit response to critics who accuse both of a kind of sociolinguistic determinism—the idea that, since Discourses are always already written, little if any agency is possible. Their argument is that literacies are always deployed within Discourses but that those literacies always have effects. Even apparently nonmainstream literacies are never simply acts of "reading." Instead, they often work within dominant Discourses for change: "[I]f you pull off a performance and it gets recognized as meaningful and appropriate in the Discourse, then it counts. That performance carries, *like a virus*, aspects of your own individuality and, too, of your other Discourses. Thus, people and their Discourses infect each other all the time" (Gee 167, emphasis added). So Discourses are not changed by conforming to them, but neither are they changed by refusing to enter them—a point Lisa Delpit has made repeatedly in defending her decision to teach features of dominant Discourses to poor children and children of color. Rather, Discourses are changed through infection.

But where Delpit would argue that novices must be invited to "enter" Discourses to shed their novitiate status and gain access to power, the negotiation seems more complex than that. Rather than always requiring newcomers to stop being newcomers, Discourses often thrive on the value novices add as well as on the disruptions they represent. Etienne Wenger has discussed the role of flexibility from the newcomer's perspective in studying communities of practice. In his empirical study, Wenger followed the training of new members of an insurance claims processing team. While it may seem to many that the work of a claims processor is fairly fixed, following rigid rules and procedures for approval and denial, for instance, Wenger found that new processors' apprenticeships instead pointed up a richly innovative community of learners balancing between the preexisting context and emergent practices. Novices, for instance, asked questions about long-standing practices that had become part of veteran members' repertoires and that went largely unnoticed, such as giving information about claims denials without a sense of the rationale behind the denial. Of course, not all emergent practices are recognized as valuable by the preexisting community. As Wenger notes, the community's inherent conservatism inflects the question of whether the new practice—and its corresponding "wisdom of peripherality" (216)—is adopted. If what the community does not (yet) do is viewed by community members as part of a trajectory of what the community could and should be, then the practice passes the adoption test. The value of emergent practice is then recognized when veteran members grant both *legitimacy* and *peripherality* to novices—that is, new members are allowed limited license to work within the community at something less than optimal performance, trading full community competence for possibly valuable innovation. And they are also kept at some (geographic or virtual) distance from the veteran members, which permits them a safe space in which to gain competence (also see Lave and Wenger).

Applying Wenger's theory of learning in community to the multilingual context of US colleges and universities uncovers both problems and possibilities. It is certainly true that multilingual English users confront a long-standing preexisting context, namely the (imagined?) community of native English users. It is also true that gaining full membership in that community requires the development and display of competence. For many, the lack of this competence means a period of compensation, which (as in the case of the claims processors) occurs at some distance from full-fledged community members and their practices. However, whereas novice processors (and many other types of workers) often have opportunities to bridge that distance with potentially valuable innovations, that opportunity is effectively foreclosed for multilingual users, for whom that distance is all but unbridgeable.

Why have the peripheral knowledges of apparently novice multilingual users not garnered more notice in composition circles? In one sense, the preexisting context of privileged forms, genres, and rhetorics constitutes for composition instructors a goal to be attained—that is, mastery of privileged forms supposedly leads to access to privilege. So maintaining the preexisting context as well as the bright-line border between multilingual users' uses and privileged uses appears to be a matter of both ethical and pragmatic responsibility. But the cost of appealing to this responsibility in apologies for standardized administrative and teaching practices is high. In fact, in Wenger's terms, it means the difference between *training* and *education*. Whereas training "aims to create an inbound trajectory targeted at competence in a specific practice, education must strive to open new dimensions for the negotiation of the self" (263). While Wenger does not directly address how messy a proposition this is, it is undoubtedly so. However, viruses love a mess. And the diverse trajectories of English's evolution are especially messy—fertile substrates for the emergence of new language practices and, arguably, pedagogies. In his article "Lingua Franca English," Suresh Canagarajah explicitly connects Lave and Wenger's practice-oriented model of learning to the learning opportunities inherent in quotidian interactions among people who use English for targeted purposes that traditional pedagogies cannot anticipate (also see "Multilingual"). Users of English as a lingua franca are typically "novices" according to long-accepted standards of English competence: at the very least, they are nonnative users of the language. They may have little cultural affinity with English and little need to learn US-centric varieties or practices. Often, as Juliane House points out, their competencies in English have more to do with specific, context-bound, interactive pragmatics than they have to do with more traditionally defined grammatical knowledge. In fact, Istvan Kecskes goes so far as to claim that English in lingua franca situations is more like a "language use mode" than a specific language variety (213). If the implied skills of interaction are indeed becoming more crucial locally and globally, *education*, not training, must point out the path to competence for *all* English users.

In the next chapters, I draw on the theoretical work laid out here to view interactions between multilingual English-speaking and monolingual native-English-speaking students in the historically sedimented but, I believe, highly productive context of first-year composition. In Chapter 2, I discuss interactions between students and teachers in regularly scheduled introductory rhetoric and composition courses. In Chapter 3, I present observations and analysis from an experimental course that paired multilingual and largely monolingual native English speakers, and I outline how that course taught me how composition can and should reorient itself. The work these students do together in writing and in other communicative forms reflects the increasingly multicultural, multilingual, and multimodal context of US and global language and rhetoric. Far from being the kind of fixed, carefully controlled, closed community of practice that multilingual English users *appear* to be required to enter, this context has benefited and will continue to benefit from the viral infections newcomers bring with them.

NOTES

1. This student's response is unedited.

2. The second definition is "a process or course of treaty with another (or others) to obtain or bring about some result." The fourth definition stresses "the action of getting over or round some obstacle by skilful maneuvering," which provides perhaps the clearest contrast to some of the uses of *negotiation* in the literature.

3. This view of student–tutor dialogue is in sharp contrast to popular notions of multiculturalism that attempt to "keep the foreign flavor alive" (Wills 9), which I read as a way of preserving cultural difference without attending to the inevitability of intercultural interaction.

4. Bakhtin's encounter with the Other is also the basis for concern about his ethical position. For Jeffrey T. Nealon, for instance, Bakhtin's "I" encounters others as part of a larger agenda of furthering the "I"'s wide-ranging subjectivity through a kind of consistent trope of exploration and colonization. I am aware of the implication of my own project in the possibility of constructing either colonial subjectivities or colonized others (or both). That is, an outcome of a pedagogy informed by my work might be an interpellation of language-learning others into service to teach monolingual-explorer-"I"s about how English works

globally, thus reversing (but not challenging) the service that one group of language learners offers another. At this time, I follow Don Bialostosky in my desire to suspend—at least temporarily—concerns about the effects of investing multilingual users with credentials as language teachers in their own right; this agency has been denied multilingual users so systematically that I am tempted to theorize about it in spite of this consequence.

5. Especially with a statement like this, I am close to the position articulated by proponents of memetics—namely, that cultural information actually replicates following its own logic and its own agenda, using human brains as hosts (see, e.g., Blackmore; Brodie; Dawkins). In this argument, the virus is not a metaphor but a close relative of the meme. At this point, I am interested in the virus's metaphorical purchase and in discussing viral *logics*, not the possible existence of cultural or linguistic replicators themselves.

2

Competence: Learning from "Learners"

> In a globalizing world, to place NNSs [nonnative English speakers] at a disadvantage when it comes to publishing their work not only goes against natural justice but is also likely to be impoverishing in terms of the creation of knowledge.
>
> —John Flowerdew

THE TWENTY-FIRST CENTURY IS NOT UNIQUE in seeing received standards of language use conflict with the messiness of encounters with apparently foreign influences. It can be instructive for current efforts to revise composition in multilingual settings to examine historical moments of multilingual English use. The emergence of conflict about language and pedagogy in Native American education of earlier periods, for instance, has received significant scholarly attention. Archival work published in anthologies of American literature (if not yet American *rhetorics*) has uncovered Native language learners who skillfully negotiated severe constraints on material provision, movement, expression, and identity. For example, in the face of carefully constrained opportunities, eighteenth-century Mohegan Christian minister and teacher Samson Occom was still able to demonstrate competence as he actively negotiated various linguistic and rhetorical traditions. Occom carved out an identity as a cultural intermediary during a time of transition in Puritan and Native American relationships in North America. For Occom, this meant articulating through autobiography, letters, and sermons a nuanced yet painfully rendered rhetorical identification with *both* Native and Puritan selves. At times, Occom gives in to the anger he feels as a result of his intermediary status. In his autobiographical "A Short Narrative of My Life," he describes his successes as a preacher and teacher for other Native Americans, but he abruptly breaks off his narrative to relate details about his and his family's material state. Even after traveling extensively in New England and the United Kingdom to raise funds for Puritan education, Occom clearly felt that he had not been appropriately remunerated. Near the end of his narrative, Occom directly accuses his Puritan teacher, Eleazar Wheelock, and other erstwhile supporters of deliberately shortchanging him, especially in comparison with an unmarried white missionary whose high support costs included a translator and "Introducer," which Occom did not need. Seemingly at the peak of his anger, Occom inserts a parenthetical self-interruption:

> Now you See what difference they made between me and other missionaries; they gave me 180 Pounds for 12 years Service, which they gave for one years Services in another Mission.— In my Service (I speak like a fool, but I am Constrained) I was my own Interpreter. I was both a School master and Minister to the Indians, yea I was their Ear, Eye & Hand, as Well as Mouth. (17–18)

Scholarly review of Occom's writing has included significant debate about this passage. Some read Occom's style here as indicating a social conflict that had become psychological: he was unable to sustain the tension between Puritan and Native identities, and his ultimate failure became clear as a failure of expression (Nelson). Other, more recent criticism interprets even this apparent breakdown in language as evidence of agency: Keely McCarthy sees here an allusion to the Christian apostle Paul's similar statement to the Corinthians. As Augustine noted in his discussion of Paul's plain language, Paul appeared to be largely uninterested in boasting. But, in Corinth, where Paul was viewed as the Christian outsider railing against "false apostles," Paul boasted about his own trials and accomplishments, apparently feeling the need to argue on the rhetorical ground that he did have:

> Are they Hebrews? So am I. Are they Israelites? So am I. Are they the seed of Abraham? So am I. Are they ministers of Christ? (I speak as a fool) I am more: in labours more abun-

dant, in stripes above measure, in prisons more frequent, in deaths oft. (2 Cor. 11.22–23, Authorized Version)

Occom may have been similarly uncomfortable with the direct, personal argument he was making but still felt impelled to make it. And in being so "Constrained"—in rhetorically identifying with and troping on the "poor Indian" his white teachers and supporters often expected—he reached out rhetorically to another outsider (McCarthy 364).

While I would not compare the dire position of Samson Occom and his family with the often privileged positions of multilingual English users in US universities today, I strongly believe that the historical, default response to Occom's writing and speaking is the same default response to the more contemporary writing and speaking of multilingual users—that is, points of apparent misunderstanding represent breaks or errors that must be eradicated, questioned, and compensated for; they rarely if ever are seen as evidence of competence and rhetorical strategy. Composition is historically tied to a sense of remediation from "error" and preparation for supposedly more advanced work in specific disciplines with their specific sets of more or less fixed competencies. And composition is often materially limited as a practice because of time constraints that make ready-made packaging of cultural and linguistic diversity attractive for instructors. These limitations put brakes on the field's ability to articulate and follow through with an expanded sense of what multilingual users may be doing with language and rhetoric.

But such brakes are untenable in the project of developing pragmatic *and* critical language users. Linguistic and rhetorical practices continue to change as they have always done—this time, aided (and sped along) by global movements of people and global shifts in markets and technologies. To disengage the brakes as fully as possible, though, rearticulations of the role of language learning (and learners) in the development of practical and critical competencies are necessary not only *in* classrooms but also *outside* them.

In one sense, the call I make here to revalue linguistic and rhetorical work as a necessarily messy, grounded, empirical practice recalls what early sociolinguists called for in the first years of the emergence of that field: for Dell Hymes, John Gumperz, and others, discovering what was situationally appropriate for anyone attempting to talk, write, and act themselves into communities was a matter for constant observation. As the empirical ideals of socio-linguistic study transformed into relatively fixed pedagogical goals, however, the insistence on open empirical study became lists of communicative norms—targets for language learners to attempt to reach. And assessment of those learners became a function of comparison between what they were able to do and what "competence" supposedly looked like. But just as English as a global and globally changing language does not—cannot—privilege one variety or one competence, the teaching of English (in foreign language courses, composition courses, and other contexts) cannot afford to continue ignoring the multiple competencies students have developed "on the ground" and often before entering their classrooms. The particular challenge for teachers, researchers, and administrators, then, is to discover (in cooperation with diverse multilingual English users) what those competencies look like and how they can be responsively and appropriately assessed and made relevant to writing pedagogy, a practice that continues to find itself at the crucial junction of students, universities, and academic and (pre)professional expression.

In this chapter, I discuss what might be called "received" concepts of competence as applied to multilingual English users and as relevant to the study and teaching of composition. I then present and analyze both published and recently collected written and spoken data that highlight multilingual users' often hidden competencies. My analysis of these data indicates the emergence of conceptual categories that make new ways of valuing these users' contributions available to themselves, their often monolingual native-English-speaking peers, their teachers, and the administrators who direct their paths through foundational course work.

COMPETENCE NEAT AND MESSY

The shift from a focus on an entirely linguistic to a more social, *communicative* competence began in the 1960s with work that responded to the cognitive linguistic theory of Noam Chomsky. In response to behaviorist explanations of language acquisition, Chomsky posited a notion of linguistic competence largely on the basis of internal cognitive capacity independent of and prior to external factors: "It appears," he writes in a sharply critical review of B. F. Skinner's behaviorist work, "that we recognize a new item as a sentence not because it matches some familiar item in any simple way, but because it is generated by the grammar that each individual has somehow and in some form internalized" (n.p.). Chomsky recognized the logistical problems of studying such internal grammars, but he theorized that their existence bridged the yawning gap between laboratory-observable experience and human language production.

For some of Chomsky's contemporaries, the methodological problem was not actually the greatest one. Much credit for articulating a third position about language learning and use goes to anthropologist and folklorist Dell Hymes. Hymes most clearly spelled out his alternative to Chomsky's cognitivist paradigm in his 1974 work, *Foundations in Sociolinguistics*, in which he focuses on "the expression of three themes that [he took] to be fundamental to sociolinguistics," including the broad organization of communities' "communicative conduct," the multidisciplinary possibilities of language study, and a revision of the bases of linguistics as a whole (vii–viii). Hymes expresses his reservations about Chomskyian allegiances between linguistics and cognitive psychology, which he fears will reinforce interest in formal language modeling. In contradiction to this trend, Hymes calls for projects that collect new language data in specific contexts to determine local patterns proper to speech activity that abstractions in grammar systems analysis might miss. Here, Hymes clearly wants to move out from under the limits "linguistics" places on what he proposes: he anticipates a descriptive science that absorbs linguistics and that sees language "situated in the flux and pattern of communicative events" (5).

Crucial to this new science is a distinction between "language" and "communication." Broader than language, which Hymes defines narrowly as linguistic code, communication comprises code, participants, an event in which they are situated, a channel, a setting, a form or shape to the message being conveyed, and a message or meaning (13). While language is obviously not dismissed, communication—with all the social context implied—is "the metaphor, or perspective, basic to rendering experience intelligible" (16). Contrary to Chomsky, whose tendency to equate linguistic code and community means for him that communities are already united by language, Hymes draws on rhetorical thinkers such as Kenneth Burke in an attempt to demonstrate the disunity of communities that cannot be theorized away. He explicitly invokes Burke's notion of identification, which he recognizes as a basic shift in rhetorical theory that mirrors the shift he was beginning to see among scholars in his own field:

> It is clear from the work of [John J.] Gumperz, [William] Labov, [Fredrik] Barth, and others that not frequency of interaction but rather definition of situations in which interaction occurs is decisive, particularly identification (or lack of it) with others. [Sociolinguistics here makes contact with the shift in rhetorical theory from expression and persuasion to identification as a key concept . . .] ("Models" 54, last brackets in original; also see *Foundations* 47)

A quantitative analysis relying on "the appearance of linguistic neatness" (47) too easily glosses over what Hymes takes to be the sociolinguist's unit of analysis: the "speech community," which he defines as "a community sharing rules for the conduct and interpretation of speech, and rules for the interpretation of at least one linguistic variety" ("Models" 54). Again, language is necessary to thinking about community, but it is not sufficient. Any quantitative analysis must be supplemented by qualitative study of the rules figured by a community as those rules define and are defined by interaction. Here, then, Hymes introduces the possibility of dynamic intragroup conflict that subverts notions of universal linguistic unity. As Gumperz notes, Hymes's focus on imperfectly realized communicative events clearly positions him against Chomsky's trouble-free "linguistic competence," which relies on a face-to-face model of interaction that does not account for social complications (Gumperz and Hymes 39).

To Chomsky's neat analytic dyad of fully "competent" native speakers, then, Hymes and his contemporaries counterposed messy communities that elude prior definition. As Constant Leung notes, little in Hymes's formulation lends itself to adoption as a set of prescriptions or proscriptions: "one has to go out, as it were, and find data to show what appropriateness is in different settings and with different participants" (131). Hymes's idea was attractive to compositionists, who characteristically found themselves defending the previously excluded students who began to populate colleges and universities after World War II and Vietnam. Sociolinguistic approaches to these students' language use promised socially grounded rationales for their apparent divergence from the mainstream as well as rigorous linguistic description of their language features—that is, there were political as well as pedagogical stakes, as the "Students' Right to Their Own Language" resolution exemplifies, and compositionists believed they had found a way simultaneously to account for and defend difference to administrators and legislators who were and are perennially interested in cutting "basic" programs.

But as important as 1960s-era sociolinguistic work was to composition, it was even more central to evolutions in foreign language teaching, which enshrined notions of language competence that have achieved broad relevance wherever English is taught. A cascade of theories, textbooks, and teachers' guides came to market in the 1970s loosely collected as part of the drive toward "communicative language teaching" (CLT). Sandra Savignon, one of the best-known articulators of this broad approach, marks the distinction between CLT and earlier, grammar- and phonology-based approaches in terms that echo Hymes's. For Savignon, the key shift is from assessing based on *norms* to assessing based on *criteria*, which "requires testers to get out from behind their desks and their 'endless word and pencil and paper games' and into the field to record and analyze actual performance" (3). Savignon relates her own experience as a teacher in a language program in which she initially felt at ease with the behavioral, repetitive, drill-based curriculum in classrooms, but where she soon came to discover that such a pedagogy did little to prepare students to produce their target language spontaneously or comfortably. Savignon and others through the 1970s developed language pedagogies that sought to infuse curricula with opportunities for students not only to hear and read "authentic" examples of their target languages but, crucially, to speak and write as well. For these teachers, *communicative* teaching meant not only learning forms but also responsively and creatively manipulating them as new language situations are met and negotiated.

Paradoxically, though, CLT's open, experiential promise becomes a victim of its own success in many classrooms worldwide. It is nearly impossible to query "communicative language teaching" or "communicative competence" in any database without finding references to Michael Canale and Merrill Swain's summary of theoretical bases (Canale; Canale and Swain). They suggest that the broad concept is reducible to four types of knowledge:

1. *Grammatical competence*, which involves familiarity with lexico-syntactic, semantic, and phonological considerations
2. *Sociolinguistic competence*, which equates to understanding the appropriateness of linguistic utterances in given contexts
3. *Discourse competence*, which refers to a language user's ability to combine utterances into recognizable and unified texts
4. *Strategic competence*, which refers to what may be seen as rhetorical abilities to compensate given uncertainty or special circumstances

Canale and Swain's list has proven to be durable: Constant Leung points to examples over the last twenty years of language textbooks and teacher materials that closely duplicate this list. Arguably, these four dimensions of learning and use represent a good cross section of desirable language learning skill, and they also represent a kind of to-do list for would-be sociolinguistic researchers interested in charting what appropriate language use looks like in communities as they evolve and co-evolve. Where this mission often fails, though, is where it meets the native speaker. Despite attacks from some critically inclined linguists (Canagarajah, "Interrogating"; Cook, "Competence," "Going Beyond"; Leung, Harris, and Rampton; Pennycook, "Disinventing"; Rampton), the shadowy figure of the native speaker—especially of English—has persisted in foreign language pedagogy to the present day. It is not unusual to see want ads for English teachers in many countries that include the phrase "native speakers only." And in fact the native speaker pops up where she or he may be least expected. In articulating a basis for assessment, numerous discussions about testing foreign language students invoke native proficiencies even where native-like production is not the ostensible goal: for at least one teacher-scholar, norms of use even in emerging English-language contexts should be based on native speaker "codification and standardness" (Sifakis 239). Yet the equation of native speaking ability with comprehensive linguistic *knowledge* is problematic. As a native speaker, I might claim linguistic competence with varieties of white, middle-class English spoken in the Southeast and Mid-Atlantic, but I am not comfortable claiming the same kind of spontaneous competence with African American Vernacular English (AAVE), even though I have studied it as a linguistic and rhetorical tradition. And even if I were linguistically competent, I might well be judged *incompetent* along any of the other three axes Canale and Swain provide if I were to use certain AAVE forms among African American friends.

Where persistent questions about linguistic standards mark discussions of competence in foreign language teaching circles, the realm of "discourse competence" marks the place where foreign language teaching, applied linguistics, and composition come most closely into contact. Another way to talk about coherence and cohesion, which are central to determining discursive abilities in the communicative paradigm, is *genre*. The concept of genre has been incredibly generative in a variety of scholarly and pedagogical strands. The tradition of English for specific purposes (ESP) views genre as a framework for introducing language learners to the common "moves" of privileged academic documents. John Swales is perhaps best known in this strand: his work identifying typical features of such research-based genres as the scientific report article has influenced writing pedagogy for native- and non-native-English-speaking graduate students (*Genre, Research*). A somewhat related approach to genre based on the systemic-functional linguistics pioneered by M. A. K. Halliday has focused on genres as "staged, goal-oriented social processes" invoked in particular situations for specific purposes (Hyon 697). This so-called Sydney school or Australian approach to language teaching resembles the ESP strand in its attention to linguistic features, but it has tended to focus on primary school genres for the purpose of providing explicit teaching to students perceived to be at a disadvantage (Cope and Kalantzis, *Powers*; Halliday and Hasan). A third strand, largely North American, lends a New Rhetoric perspective that seeks to explain genre as linked to social action (Carolyn Miller). In this strand, discrete moves in generic documents are taken to be less important than analyzing—often through ethnographic rather than textual methods—how genres respond to social exigencies and rhetorical situations (Freedman and Medway; Herrington and Moran), as well as how they mediate communities and their activities (Berkenkotter and Huckin).

While there are key differences among strands in genre studies, especially over the issue of whether and how to teach generic forms and moves explicitly, there are also points of agreement and cross-influence. For instance, it would be hard to find a genre theorist who disagreed with Anne Herrington and Charles Moran's observation that genre has historical roots nearly as deep as those of thought itself. And many theorists across strands would also agree with Richard Coe, Lorelei Lingard, and Tatiana Teslenko that genre often involves both rhetorical shaping of knowledge communities and rhetorical persuasion. What I am most interested in, however, is how two strands—ESP and the New Rhetoric—appear to be evolving in recent work, because their developments suggest a crisis in thinking about genre and cultural and linguistic diversity. They also suggest a productive way forward that theorists outside of genre studies have begun to take up more forcefully.

The crisis appears precisely at the interface between where students came from and where they enter colleges and universities. I have already recalled Richard Ohmann's observation that composition pedagogy—especially as represented in the field's textbooks—has tended to assume that students arrive in classrooms with little prior preparation as writers or as critical users of language. In past years, this premise formed the basis for teaching that attempted to eradicate the supposedly bad influences that life outside the academy had on students' habits, but more recently, it has provided support for the argument that classrooms are the best and only spaces to place students' home languages/vernacular literacies/folkways alongside more academic/formal/public literacies in order to achieve critical perspectives. Some work in genre provides good examples. In her 2004 book *Writing Genres*, Amy J. Devitt expresses some discomfort with the New Rhetoric's tradition of critiquing the explicit teaching of genre. In words that echo Lisa Delpit's famous argument about explicit teaching to disadvantaged students, Devitt cautions that moving away from explicit teaching entirely risks failing to expose students to the ideological functions of genre—that is, leaving off teaching the forms might mean that students do not develop the ability to recognize them and manipulate them for their own discursive ends.[1] "Of course," as she points out, "knowing how to learn new genres may also have been learned without explicit instruction," which is an admission that students may have acquired pragmatic and critical genre knowledge outside and before the classroom. However, Devitt directly questions "the extent of that learning," thus locating *efficacious* genre teaching firmly in the US college classroom (195). Rochelle Kapp and Bongi Bangeni, writing about teaching argumentative composition to students in South Africa, go quite a bit further (and, arguably, further backward). Their experiences with Black students entering the University of Cape Town for the first time from previously excluded communities leads them to believe that those students "have to negotiate a chasm that is not only cognitive and linguistic in character, but also social and affective" (110). Their characterization of this "chasm" and of the apparently worthless literacies on the *wrong* side of it leads them to exclude much mention of students who "were still writ[ing] in a mainly oral register" and who "wrote personal narratives that avoided the theory." Instead, they focus their attention and their transcriptions on students who "grappled with argument construction" (121). I do not want to downplay the value to these students of learning academic argument conventions or of the struggles they handled while attempting to become critical students, both of which Kapp and Bangeni compellingly present. I do, however, mean to question what was really happening with the outliers—the students whose performances Kapp and Bangeni effectively silence because they were failing to meet the requirements of the scholars' critical-academic pedagogy. What value might these students—who *may* have been resisting the pedagogy, who *may* have had something to add from their "oral" backgrounds that might have helped them, their peers, and their teachers negotiate their movements between home and school—have added to the course if their teachers had been willing to suspend judgment?

I have already written about the value I foresee in suspending judgment—in slowing the moment of response and even assessment to allow for the presentation of potentially productive misunderstandings. But I return to the notion here to mark what I see as an opening in genre theory and in related studies—one that has led me to my own developing empirical work. As closely as John Swales has been associated with a kind of top-down, concrete, teacherly analysis of discrete moves in research genres, it is Swales who provides perhaps the clearest articulation of how genre studies has to orient itself to changes in language and rhetoric going forward. In a reappraisal of his 1990 work *Genre Analysis*, Swales qualifies the "climbing an academic ladder" metaphor he has proposed in the past by calling attention to how technology and culture are spreading, changing, and mutually informing each other. Perhaps the most telling example he cites is English itself. Swales notes the number and growth of nonnative English speakers in many disciplines, including the sciences and applied linguistics, which—at least, practically speaking—gives the lie to the native–nonnative dichotomy and to exclusions that follow from it (*Research*).

For Swales, the relevant distinction going forward will be based less on nativeness of English and more on broadness of proficiency. He envisions a shift in terminology from *NS* (native-speaking) versus *NNS* (non-native-speaking) to *broadly* and *narrowly* English-proficient. He argues that such a shift makes the following scenario possible:

> Those with English as an L2 may still evince minor grammatical and lexical oddities, may be less than fully colloquial in their speech, and may have "unusual" pronunciation features of various sorts, but, especially if of SR [senior academic] status, will likely have rhetorical and procedural competencies that are considerably more developed than [those of] junior researchers with English as their L1. (*Research* 57)

The categories Swales proposes necessitate difficult questions about what competence means in research settings: after all, Swales himself sees this new dichotomy as little more than an initial stab, gesturing to other "graduated competencies" that would provoke more nuanced assessments (*Research* 56). And those questions could only become more complicated *outside* Swales's relatively narrow focus on academic research writing. In other words, what happens when the mixing of different English users whom Swales points to in academic circles becomes even more pronounced in the countless other academic and professional endeavors US college undergraduates will engage in?

The answer may well lie in the original impetus behind much of the sociolinguistic work that occasioned both CLT and genre theory: empirical research. Hymes's articulation of communicative competence outlined an empirical program that required augmenting, if not replacing, general analyses of linguistic "competence" with assessments of "performance" within local social bounds (*Foundations*). It is a short leap from discovering and making available these measures of performance to reifying them as more or less timeless targets for language learners. So the necessary complement to this empirical focus is empirical *grounding* that continues situational research on communicative contexts while keeping codification at bay.

REGROUNDING CONCEPTIONS OF COMPETENCE

In the remaining portions of this chapter, I turn to English language learners' emerging competencies as they appear in published literature and in my own empirical study. My approach to analyzing these competencies is based on grounded theory (GT), a longstanding orientation in social sciences and health studies that in recent years has also affected (largely qualitative) research in other fields closer to my own (see especially Neff). Since its original articulation by Barney Glaser and Anselm Strauss in 1967, GT has undergone some modification, including a bifurcation into argumentative camps.[2] However, it is still possible to generalize several principles of GT:

1. "Open coding" of data into categories that honor and reflect as far as possible both the researcher's and the participants' perspectives.

2. "Axial coding" that reflects the constant comparison of incoming data with previously gathered data and that reflects a refinement of developing categories.

3. Continuing data collection up to "saturation"—a point at which incoming data no longer suggest necessary additional categories and at which a "theory" accounting for the data "emerges."

Recent refinements of GT, including Strauss and Corbin's, reinforce a balance between etic (researcher-originated) and emic (participant-originated) perspectives (Pike; also see Canagarajah, "Lingua Franca"): they recognize the value of published literature in suggesting "sensitizing concepts" that may be operationalized in GT or in providing evidence of gaps in research that GT may be employed to fill (Charmaz; Strauss and Corbin). Further refinement of GT in light of postmodern theories has attempted to expand GT's traditional scope from a preoccupation with a community's "basic social process" to an appreciation of other factors that impinge on the community's interactions, such as the institutional power structures that influence composition (Clarke; Strauss and Corbin).

I see considerable value in using GT to ground empirical research on evolving English-language practices. Foremost, the approach's focus on ongoing data collection and recursive refinement of analytical claims seems instrumental in forestalling the establishment of a final, fixed set of competencies. (As diverse English practices proliferate, it seems unlikely that GT researchers would reach a saturation point beyond which no new competencies could be articulated.) Second, the approach's relative flexibility in data collection, which permits the inclusion of both published reports and empirical observations, allows researchers to analyze a wide variety of examples representing several fields that study multilingual users. Third, the approach's insistence on foregrounding participants' own analysis reinforces the idea that language users should be conscious of language practices as they occur.

My data include fifteen publications[3] in the fields of second language composition, rhetoric and composition, and applied linguistics. They also include audio-recorded and/or field-notated interactions among second-language- and native-English-speaking students and teachers in approximately ten sections of first-year composition at three large public universities in the Mid-Atlantic, Southeast, and Intermountain West, as well as follow-up interviews with select students and instructors.[4] While I recognize the problems of relying on other researchers' published representations of their data, I view their inclusion as essential to my project of articulating a new set of assumptions about multilingual users. These published accounts provide the "raw" material for the development of a set of sensitizing concepts that I have taken into my own empirical research—to date, I have been unable to find any published work that has attempted a meta-analytical reading of this collection or similar collections of research articles as representatives of an overall effort to chart multilingual users' competencies. My choice of these articles is necessarily selective, but I believe they represent a good cross section of work that spans time, disciplinary divisions, and educational contexts. I also take seriously the tenet of contemporary, constructivist GT that values my experience as a researcher as much as it values the experiences of my participants. In taking my own experience seriously, I am guided by Claire Kramsch's sensitivity to what she terms "telling moments"—"my misunderstanding of a student's utterance, an unusual silence, a student's unexpected reaction, a grammatical or lexical mistake that doesn't make sense" ("From Practice" 197). I am also guided by Joyce Magnotto Neff's articulation of "notable moments" in GT projects, in which the teacher-researcher is alerted to "things which jump out at me *because of*, not in spite of, my experience" (129, emphasis in original).

My observations coupled with my analysis of select published literature have suggested many categories for further research and refinement. Several of these categories resemble Canale and Swain's list of communicative competencies. However, some point to new competencies that linguistic and communicative approaches do not presently anticipate. Although numerous competencies have emerged from my recursive readings of the growing data set,[5] I list and describe here the competencies that appear in multiple sources (especially in *both* publications and my observations) and/or those that emerge so far most persistently. So I focus on the following competencies not only to provide a relatively limited sample for the sake of economy but also, and more crucially, to limit further analysis to those competencies most likely to hold up under future data collection because of their consistent appearance already across the data set:

1. "Book" knowledge of English grammar
2. Lexical and syntactic innovation
3. Linguistic and/or rhetorical resistance/accommodation
4. Cross-cultural information/critique
5. Meta-task orientation
   a. Meta-discursive sensitivity
   b. Group dynamic sensitivity

"Book" Knowledge of English Grammar

Second language pedagogy has historically assumed that learners learn best in a grammar-heavy curriculum (Benesch; Matsuda,

"Second"; Savignon). Even though the communicative approach to language teaching and more recent, sociocultural approaches (see, e.g., Lantolf and Thorne) counterpose more interactive pedagogies, textbook-based grammar-translation methods are still prevalent. The widespread distribution of these methods through English-as-a-foreign-language courses abroad means that teachers and researchers can safely assume that their truly "foreign" students develop a relatively high level of grammatical meta-knowledge—especially compared to native speakers of the target language. While Joy Reid stops well short of labeling their knowledge as a kind of "competence," she categorizes many foreign English-language students as "eye learners" whose oral discomfort in English masks grammatical knowledge and whose "errors" in written English may actually point to attempts to overcorrect for grammar. Even before Reid's influential article appeared, anecdotal knowledge about foreign language learners seemed right in line with her analysis. During my Peace Corps service, for instance, I could muddle through explanations of why Polish nouns were declined the way they were in different sentences when my Polish friends had no idea, and my native Polish students were much more adept than I was at discussing English-language conditionals.

A limited number of research articles has called attention to otherwise unexpected or unnoticed competencies of this kind—competencies that may be called into service for both learners and supposed "experts." In a widely cited article, Min-Zhan Lu discusses one of her (native-Chinese-speaking) students' deployment of the term *can able to* to emphasize *both* external permission to do something *and* internal ability—a use supported by the student's careful reading of an English dictionary. The difference in meaning between *can* and *to be able to* that gives rise to the student's use represents a distinction often lost in common (US) usage but one that had real value for a student attempting to come to terms with her Chinese- and English-speaking identities:

> Most native English speakers among my students tend to argue that in actual usage, only grandmas and schoolteachers make the distinction between "can" and "may." *Everyone*

uses "can" and "be able to" interchangeably nowadays. In response, I tell them the writer's position on the issue. She was aware of the distinction—she was the one who first called my attention to definition 5 [of *can* in *The Random House Dictionary*]. (Lu, "Professing" 451–52, emphasis in original)

Other articles point to knowledge that makes nonnative English users adept teachers and even editors. Péter Medgyes has produced articles and a book that detail non-native-English-speaking teachers' unique skills. George Braine's collection on nonnative teachers includes contributions by nonnative English users Suresh Canagarajah, Ulla Connor, Claire Kramsch, and other notable scholars in second language writing and language acquisition—many of whom claim, as Medgyes puts it, "abundant knowledge about and insight into how the English language works, which might be presumed to make them better informants than their native colleagues" (347). While the claim that such teachers may also be uniquely effective in courses enrolling *native*-English-speaking students has not yet been made, John Flowerdew uncovers a welcoming attitude on the part of at least some editors of international publications. In interviews with several editors of journals in applied linguistics and international English-language teaching, Flowerdew notes, among others, one editor's opinion that "nonnative grammarians tend to be very good. And historically, we just have to look at the grammarians of the English language, and most of them are NNSs. They can bring an objectivity to a task that many NSs won't be able to" (qtd. in Flowerdew 143). The emergence of these opinions might mark a shift from a view of second language users as linguistically competent *among other second language users* to a view of their competencies as more generally viable, even in the relatively linguistically conservative realm of academic publishing.

Lexical and Syntactic Innovation

Lexical divergences from expected English norms are often the easiest differences for so-called native speakers and writers to detect, and they are often the first frontier of misunderstanding. But they do not have to be. In fact, the lexical innovations that multilingual users employ may even lead to more elegant and locally appropriate language. In a TESOL plenary address, Henry Widdowson relates the Indian English example of *prepone,* which is, on its face, awkward, but which merely reflects a common innovative practice—albeit in a less-than-privileged way:

> Take, for example, the two words *depone* and *prepone.* The first is a technical legal term and therefore highly respectable. The second[,] *prepone*[,] is not. It is an Indian English word of very general currency, coined to contrast with *postpone.* To postpone an event means to put it back; to prepone an event is to bring it forward. The coinage exploits the morphology of English in an entirely regular way. It is apt. But it is also quaint. An odd Indian excrescence: obviously nonstandard. And yet there is clearly nothing deviant in the derivational process itself, and indeed we can see it at work in the formation of the related words *predate* and *postdate.* But these are sanctioned as entirely ordinary, proper, standard English words. What, then, is the difference? The difference lies in the origin of the word. *Prepone* is coined by a nonnative-speaking community, so it is not really a proper English word. It is not pukka. And of course the word *pukka* is itself only pukka because the British adopted it. (383–84)

In this example, lexical innovation results from the regular application of a rule involving prefixes. Lu presents a more complex example. She writes of the emergence of "collecting money toilets" in Beijing—a phenomenon that has been derided by local, regional, and national Chinese newspapers as "Chinglish" gone especially bad. There is little doubt that many visitors (especially Western, native-English-speaking visitors) would be jarred on seeing this sign when expecting the more common Western "public" toilet. There is also little doubt about local, regional, and national sensitivities to such apparent errors before, during, and after the 2008 Summer Olympics. But it is difficult to settle on a reading of "collecting money toilet" as mere error in view of the historical valence that the standardized Chinese equivalent of *public* carries. Lu's explanation highlights the circulation of one of the Chinese phonetic characters for *public* alongside other characters to signify "communism" during the Maoist-era Great Leap Forward ("Essay" 29). Even assuming that the sign maker had little or no conventional competence in English beyond that needed to translate Chinese characters using a dictionary, Lu points out numerous factors at play that may nonetheless have prompted sophisticated choices: the sign maker, for instance, may have heard and seen the "public" character associated with communism in her youth; she may be sensitive to current sociolinguistic trends that make language about the "public" unfashionable; or she may have grown up using another variety of Chinese altogether, which would cause her to feel uncertain about translating from standardized Chinese in the first place (29–30). In any event, Lu's (perhaps charitable) readings of what the sign maker in question may have been doing at least raises the question of lexical *choice* instead of *limitation*.

Such choice is actually thrown into sharper relief in examples of Chinese name taking. Many US teachers have anecdotal experience with students who report English-language "equivalents" to their Chinese names that provoke smiles—if not laughter. Often, name-taking practices seem to track circulations of US popular culture so that students arrive in classes with iconic names of movie stars, cartoon characters, and musicians. More than just a statement of assimilation or cultural knowledge, though, such naming may suggest multifaceted attempts to claim identities:

> They look for names that serve multiple, often conflicting language affiliations and visions of self to help them gain access to all the countries of the world, to call attention to "a side of them that eats McDonald's and listens to George Michael," to increase their chances of being remembered and thus promoted by "foreign bosses," to give them "personality in a sometimes impersonal society," to continue the Chinese tradition of placing great stock in the meaning of names, or to reject the tradition of name-picking left from China's earlier encounters with Western missionaries and colonizers. So instead of picking standardized English names like Mary, Agnes,

Peter, or John, Zhao Tianqi, an artist whose woodblock prints have been selling well to foreigners, has named himself Colour Zhao. Wang Lei, a video editor, has opted for a literal translation of his birth name, Lei, and goes around Beijing as Thunder Wang. Others have claimed Western brands, calling themselves Kodak or Levi. (Lu, "Essay" 23–24)

Linguistic and/or Rhetorical Resistance/Accommodation

As the name-changing example clearly illustrates, lexical innovations are often more than just novel ways to express meaning where English does not quite fit. Names are never just names—they speak to affiliations across time and space (for instance, with others who have similar names) far more effectively than they suggest the purported "historical" meanings listed in books of baby names for new parents. Lu claims that naming calls to mind both accommodation to Western attempts to convert and colonize *and* resistance to Western influence. I am reminded here of Native American students' attempts to negotiate their own resistance and accommodation during several hundred years of missionary and reservation education—some of which I discussed earlier and which appears in the historical work of Jessica Enoch, Scott Richard Lyons, Richard Morris, and Malea Powell. I also note other examples of complex attempts to accommodate and resist, involving both immediate classroom-based power relationships and more overtly political relationships surrounding classrooms. I categorize these examples as "linguistic and/or rhetorical" to highlight the fact that they involve some linguistic adoptions and adaptations but in an overall context of response to particular situations. Thus, they involve nonlinguistic, paralinguistic, or other symbolic strategies as well.

Multilingual students often encounter assignments based on teachers' and programs' assumptions about who they are and where they come from. Notably, US-resident students may be asked to write about experiences in their "home countries," prompting them to write about Philadelphia, New York City, or one of thousands of other communities across *this* country. In other situations, multilingual users may respond to these and other assignments that require cultural analysis by leveraging their perceived status as out-siders. In two studies directly focusing on this phenomenon, Linda Harklau and Ilona Leki tally a range of strategies students call on to cope with often inconsistent and unclear expectations in several educational settings. Leki provides the example of Ling, who con-sistently acts as a kind of cultural informant in writing assignments for her courses:

> [T]he strategy that Ling used most effectively was taking ad-vantage of first language/culture by relying on her special sta-tus as an international student. As the semester went on, she attempted to incorporate something about China or Taiwan into every piece of writing she did, saying, "I am Chinese. I take advantage." Thus, her term paper in Behavioral Geog-raphy became a comparison of ancient Chinese and Greek education and this despite her history professor's direct re-quest that she not focus yet again on China. In this case she used a combined strategy of resisting the professor's request and of reliance on her special status as a Chinese person, and it worked. (Leki, "Coping" 242)

Apparently, Ling not only uses her perspective to provide rhetori-cal material for writing, but she also distributes this material across courses when a given course's "market" for it is more or less tapped out. In her longitudinal study of students transitioning from high school to college, Linda Harklau notes that markets for narratives relating the immigrant experience are rarely if ever tapped out, meaning that some multilingual users may use immigration *topoi* as a recurring resource:

> [A]lthough the sentiments expressed in Aeyfer's autobiogra-phy may have been genuine, at the same time her teacher was perhaps unaware that Aeyfer had been asked to produce vir-tually the same narrative by at least two previous teachers and had probably received similar reactions. . . . In fact, the power of such narratives to arouse sympathy and admiration created significant incentives for students to disclose such narratives even when not explicitly solicited by teachers. For example,

in response to the fairly broad and open-ended essay prompt, "Give an account of an event that actually happened or that you imagined," Claudia told the story of how she had been singled out for harassment by U.S.-born peers as a newcomer in elementary school. (48)

At times, rather than leveraging cultural information, students may leverage local support systems or even create such systems where they might not exist. Leki discusses Tula, a graduate student who uses her interactions with a course teaching assistant to develop a successful formal strategy in response to what turns out to be a rhetorically restrictive assignment:

> The teacher had developed an elaborate and carefully prepared description of the assignment, which included, among other things, the requirement to list at least five of the researchers' basic assumptions. Tula was quite pleased with the evaluation of her first attempt at writing, 16 points out of a possible 20, but realized that she had lost the 4 points on the section of her review that called for an analysis of those basic assumptions. . . . When Tula went to see the teaching assistant (TA) for the course, the TA simply advised her to use the words *assume* or *assumption* throughout that section. When I asked Tula again after the professor's corrections and after her conference with the TA what the professor meant by asking the students to identify the research article's basic assumptions, she said she was still unable to grasp what the professor was getting at, but from then on Tula included in each article review the word *assume* or *assumption*, and from then on she received full credit for her answers. ("Coping" 243–44)

Other students may take advantage of classroom space and arrangements to get feedback serendipitously:

> This strategy included not only feedback on their own work but the feedback that in one way or another they noticed their NES [native-English-speaking] classmates receiving from the teacher, either publicly and orally in class or on their written assignments, which several of the participants managed to

surreptitiously gain access to (by looking over shoulders and across aisles). (Leki, "Coping" 249)

These subtle, opportunistic strategies often appear outside of classrooms, as well. One student I observed and interviewed related several different ways she gauges whether to use English or Korean around interlocutors who may use either. For this student and for many others, the choice of which language to use is more complicated than simply code-switching: the social stakes are high, and the immediate, short-term social consequences of choosing incorrectly may be negative. This student may wait for someone in the group to take a turn at speaking (in one language or the other, as if to set the script and the stage) or pretend that she doesn't know the language at first, resisting her own ability to communicate in favor of "try[ing] to get past the awkward moment." In and out of classrooms, then, students deploy not only multilingual but also subtle *rhetorical* strategies, including (at least formalistic) accommodation to situational demands as well as resistance to a range of expected academic and social behaviors.

Cross-Cultural Information/Critique

Multilingual students' subtle accommodation and resistance to academic and social scripts certainly carry political tones. But these students also more directly stake out ground based on their intercultural positions. Unlike Ling's strategy of calling on her status as Chinese to provide diverse *topoi* for assignments, this cross-cultural strategy involves calling on prior experiences in order to challenge local beliefs and practices and/or throw local assumptions and knowledges into relief. At times this strategy may complement communicative partners' strategies, for instance in formal or informal ethnographic studies. Paul Matsuda and Tony Silva report on students' activities during a cross-cultural composition class at Purdue University that enrolled equal numbers of multilingual and monolingual native-English-speaking students. In one situation, two students representing different cultural and language backgrounds worked together to analyze a conversation that neither could have fully appreciated separately:

Nathan, a US student, and Stephanie, an Indonesian student, observed a group of Indonesian students meeting regularly for lunch in the student union. Since Nathan did not understand the Indonesian language, he concentrated on describing nonverbal behavior—which was more transparent to the Indonesian student—while Stephanie acted as a cultural informant. (21)

In other situations, multilingual users bring experience and knowledge to bear in more overtly confrontational ways that may have repercussions beyond particular interactions. Students' reporting on their experiences may not only encourage them to contribute more actively in the future but may also prompt new directions for dialogue and new rhetorical strategies for other students. Numerous composition classrooms with a rhetorical or current events bent have included discussions of the government's response to Hurricane Katrina and of efforts to renew and revise the USA PATRIOT Act. One instructor I interviewed, Cynthia,[6] related an exchange between her basic writing students[7] over the merits of relocating New Orleans residents to the city's Superdome in the days after the hurricane, prompting a personal response from a Liberian student:

> So when Katrina happened, [this student] was very distressed. Very distressed. And the class was talking about it and we were reading some of the online blogs I had them read—talking about what people were saying. And one of the students in class made the comment, "Well, it was better to—at least they were living in a big sports stadium instead of being on the street. I don't know what the big deal is," that kind of thing. . . . And [the Liberian student] said, "It's never good. It's never good to go to a place like that." And the students said, "Well yeah, it's better than nothing," but she said, "No," and she went on and explained how for two years she lived in what was supposed to be a temporary place. And the students were moved. Visibly moved by her story—and all of a sudden had a context they didn't understand before. They had no understanding that, you know, what does "temporary" mean?

. . . And it was an extraordinary time, and after that, she never was quiet again. It was just unbelievable—before that never said a word and I never requested [her to] because I knew she was uncomfortable speaking in the class, but the manner in which the students questioned her and listened to what she had to say and how it made sense because it was so directly connected to this experience they were trying to understand changed things dramatically.

Cynthia reported another interaction—this time in an honors first-year composition course—over the effects of the Patriot Act on international telephone calls and travel:

And one of the young men in class said he just didn't understand what the big deal was—that we needed to get terrorists, and whatever way we needed to get them, that was enough. . . . And finally [the student] from the [United Arab] Emirates said, "You can't understand how somebody else could feel, because you don't call your mother and your father on a daily basis the way I do"—and I think they're living in Pakistan now—[inaudible]. And then a native speaker in class who happened to have a Pakistani roommate who came from— who was like, none of this made any sense to her until, she said, she had a roommate who was an international student. She said, "I identify with that—her parents call and she calls on a daily basis. Does that mean that her phone could be tapped?" And so all of a sudden, there was this personal level of conversation, and the young man who made the statement said, "Well, that couldn't happen to you—you have nothing to hide. Only people that have things to hide should be concerned." He [the student from the UAE] goes, "How do you know I have nothing to hide?"

Hopeful arguments about the power of first-year composition courses to challenge students' opinions have long persisted, often predicated on the belief that students will respond to entirely textual presentations of cultural and linguistic differences. In these examples, though, students confronted other students with their different experiences face to face, which appears to open the possibility of new topics and new approaches.

> Students would check in with each other in their discussions, and they would say, "Well, I've never experienced that but, well, what do you think" kind of thing, so all of a sudden they began to recognize that, gee, maybe their worldview worked for them, but it may not necessarily work for someone else, so you know I don't want to say it was like this vast change of "Oh, everybody changed," no, but I would say that the benefit that came about was this willingness now to check in, this willingness to look at somebody else and say, "Well, I don't know, it doesn't seem like a big deal to me, but is that a big deal?"

Meta-task Orientation

While I would argue that second language students' abilities to shift rhetorical ground in composition classrooms—to answer the question "Is that a big deal?" in often unexpected ways—is certainly an intriguing and important competency, many teachers may wonder what positive effect, if any, second language users have on specific assignments. Joy Reid and Barbara Kroll have noted that multilingual users' responses to assignment prompts in a variety of courses across the curriculum can highlight idiomatic or vague language, unclear objectives, and ambiguous assessment criteria. Beyond identifying problems with assignment design, multilingual users may display strategies in oral and written feedback with peers that affect group dynamics and assignment focus. I observed two sets of interactions involving students in different sections of first-year composition, and I interviewed the teachers of both sections as well as frequent peer collaborators of one of the students. While neither of the multilingual users in these sections responded to my requests for out-of-class interviews, their instructors and peers corroborated my observations that they responded very differently to peer review sessions. The female student, Melanie, a native Chinese speaker and US resident, was actively engaged in several peer review sessions I observed, making both approving and critical comments and recording those comments on the worksheets the teacher supplied. The male student, Tran, a Vietnamese American first-generation college student, was much more reticent in peer review sessions, making relatively few comments.

Despite their differences, however, I noted similarities in their approaches that suggest sensitivity to—and willingness to intervene on the basis of—needing to get assignment-related tasks done in group settings. What I am referring to as these students' "meta-task orientation" actually manifests itself in two ways: attention to meta-discourse both in written drafts and in oral and written feedback, and attention to moving group dialogue along productively.

Meta-discursive Sensitivity

In the peer review sessions I observed Melanie participate in, as well as in the comments made by her peers and instructor, I had the clear impression that she was seriously invested in working productively and efficiently. In Melanie's class, the instructor directed peer review through the use of worksheets that prompted reviewers' attention to purpose and audience, claims and other argument characteristics, and grammar. For the most part, Melanie did not seem to address grammar, focusing instead on connections between evidence and claims as well as on transitions and other meta-discursive features. In fact, the instructor of this section was pleased that Melanie "didn't get caught up in grammar" and that she pointed out characteristics of her own and her peers' writing that were "beyond the obvious."[8] While Melanie's instructor did not elaborate on what this meant, Melanie's frequent peer collaborators gave a sense that she consistently made comments that probed for alternative arguments and for elaboration:

> I think basically when she—first of all, when I get [the paper] back, there's maybe like one thing underlined or something, like she doesn't go through and do grammar and things like that, when most people would look through and try and re-structure sentences and things like that. But what she's good about is she will tell me like if my idea—it's mostly she worries about the idea of the paper and like if I'm letting it come

across well enough, she'll suggest other ways I could do that, but she doesn't really worry so much about the paragraphs themselves or how the like the writing is, but she's good at like suggesting alternatives and making sure that my idea comes across. (Carla)

[O]n the last writing that she did for me that she proofread for me, she gave me really good feedback on one paragraph in particular, saying that she didn't think that I had given enough evidence to support my topic, and she found an actual case where I think—I can't remember the exact case, but I remember it was for whether or not summer school could be a stress relief, and she gave actual—she found a way to refute it, she said you should definitely include information to counteract for this response. So that was wonderful. (Lisa)

Carla mentioned that she, Melanie, and their third partner, Lisa, seemed to work together well as a system, with each member focusing on different points of critique as if to distribute workload:

Lisa, who I also do it with a lot, she mostly like corrects sentences, tells me what sentences are awkward and things like that, so when I get a paper back from her it's covered with like suggestions for how to fix the sentences. When—she still kind of touches on like the ideas, but it kind of works well for me because I get like the grammar from one person and then more of the ideas from another.

Melanie's insistence on suggesting alternatives, counterarguments, and balanced evidence seemed to carry over into a more generalized pattern of response. Many of her oral and written comments in this and other peer groups included articulations of positive and more critical comments, with clear meta-discursive shifts from one to another—no matter how rushed the sessions were. (In some cases, I observed Melanie quickly and intently reading through peers' drafts and sketching sometimes incomplete comments on worksheets in attempts to finish with one group and move on to the next in the fifty minutes allotted for class.) In one interaction with a classmate writing a definition of the term *cowboy,* Melanie characteristically shifted from a positive appraisal of her peer's strategy of comparing *knight* and *cowboy* to a critical comment about needing more transition words in order to avoid an "abrupt" "strong transition." Later, Melanie used a clear verbal transition herself in relating her peer's "other problem," re-creating stereo-typical images of cowboys through his lengthy physical description of a kind of Marlboro Man. Her meta-task focus was also apparent on the worksheets that she (sometimes hurriedly) completed: on this peer's and on a fellow L2 user's, Melanie consistently recycled keywords from the worksheet prompts, writing "aim:"; "audience:"; and "tone/style:" as if to reinforce prompts for her feedback.

Perhaps the clearest example of Melanie's task orientation appeared in her brief interaction with Scott, a male, native-English-speaking peer with whom she worked on drafts of the class's evaluation argument paper. Scott wrote what he apparently intended as a humorous take on the "paper or plastic?" question that grocery shoppers are often asked. In the introduction to his short draft, he presented several fictional accounts of paper versus plastic debates since the days of the Byzantine Empire. It was unclear how far Scott intended to carry this line of argument/narrative, since, as he put it to Melanie as she finished reading his draft, he "kind of wrote it out this morning—sorry." Possibly because their review session was occurring near the end of class time, Melanie seemed especially eager to give Scott feedback and to be direct:

> M: What's your intention with this paper?
>
> S: I should try to create an introduction that explains my intention more.
>
> M: Only concern I have about this is that it's evaluation paper and [inaudible] shouldn't be a history paper. [pause] Yeah, it seems more like discussion paper than evaluation paper. Maybe you wanna say why paper is better or why plastic is better. Maybe put the thesis in introduction, because like right here it's paper versus plastic—you're just talking about history.
>
> S: . . . The evil empire, yeah.

Melanie either did not understand Scott's attempt at humor or she understood the attempt and was trying to convey that he had little time for humor—especially humorous fictional writing that did not meet the assignment—namely, to take a side and argue evaluatively. While it is unclear from this interchange whether Scott fully intended to take Melanie's advice, he was aware—judging by his self-deprecation—that the draft had gaps. Melanie, meanwhile, laid out a quick and arguably formulaic plan for Scott to follow, consisting of clarifying his claim, arranging it in the introduction, and providing supporting reasons—in short, a distillation of the advice that my observations of the course overall indicated their instructor had given them. Assuming Scott received subsequent feedback from other class peers, he may well have been encouraged in his attempt at humor, which would replicate the effect of the system Melanie worked in with her other peers, Carla and Lisa. It is arguable that maintaining a humorous perspective in this paper could have helped Scott, since his instructor would soon be reading twenty-four evaluation papers that would likely follow a conventional thesis-support arrangement. In this early stage, however, Melanie's advice to Scott at least had the effect of focusing their attention on the essentials of what Scott's argument paper should do. In this regard, Melanie's advice reflects a recommendation from Dwight Atkinson and Vai Ramanathan's study of cultural differences between L2 and L1 composition. The study revealed that multilingual composition courses were much more focused on the development of rhetorical forms than putatively mainstream courses were. In fact, Atkinson and Ramanathan found that mainstream instructors preferred that students avoid formulaic, five-paragraph-theme writing in favor of developing more creatively arranged essays. However, Atkinson and Ramanathan argue that multilingual students may at least initially benefit from carrying strategies over as a rhetorical starting point for more advanced compositions. Data in my study suggest further that, to the extent that multilingual users focus on traditional, essayistic rhetorical forms, they may be well equipped not only to develop their own writing from a familiar base but also to provide efficient feedback for their peers.

Group Dynamic Sensitivity

In many ways, Tran's interactions with his peers in another section of composition could not have been more different from Melanie's. Whereas Melanie was talkative, clearly task oriented, and often intensely focused on providing balanced feedback, Tran was reserved—at times, barely speaking at all during sessions I observed and recorded. It is important to note that Tran's instructor was clear during her interview with me about his lack of overall participation, but she frequently qualified her specific comments about Tran with comments about the low level of participation in the class as a whole. She was uncertain whether the 8:00 a.m. class time was a primary reason or whether there were other factors, but she was direct about saying that Tran was not her class's least contributing member.

In fact, despite his comparative reticence, Tran exhibited his own brand of meta-task behavior that appeared to maintain the rhythm of two groups during their peer response tasks. After each of his contributions, the rest of the members of each group changed topics, moving further through the essays under review. In the first group of the day, with four students, two students debated whether the draft they were reading should include the colloquial rhetorical question "What the heck?" if it is intended for publication as a letter to a newspaper editor. The students expressed some uncertainty, and Tran interjected: "I think it's good to leave it there, though, because she's writing to a college age [pause] that wouldn't really care much." The other students verbally assented ("hmm . . . yeah"), and the group moved on to the next paragraph. In the second group, also with four students, Tran fielded a direct question from the author of a draft under review about whether she needed to support a statistical claim about a US state's population: "I think so—it'd be nice to support some of the sentence, yeah." Again, two other group members assented ("It couldn't hurt," "I think you're right"). In reading the group's second paper under review, Tran argued that one of the sentences was too long and should be split, asserting, "No one's going to read it if it's this long." The other three group members assented and laughed, and then everyone paused for approximately thirty seconds before moving on to another part of the letter.

Tran's contributions to these peer groups were no doubt subtle. But the connection between his brief comments and the development of his peer groups' conversational dynamics around the drafts they were reviewing appear too coincidental not to note. In addition, the letter-to-the-editor assignment was one that specifically engaged Tran's literacy experiences: in my classroom observations, I frequently noticed him reading sections of the campus newspaper. His summative comment that one writer's draft included sentences that were too long may be read as rhetorically competent in its own right in addition to pragmatically competent as a topic transition. Much work in multilingual composition has focused on tailoring peer review experiences for the benefit of second language users. It appears that this work could stand to be updated to account for second language users' group competencies.

CONCLUSION

I have presented a sampling of consistently observed multilingual user competencies ranging from lexical and grammatical knowledge, which has provided a basis for published arguments about the value of nonnative speakers as teachers and even editors, to cross-cultural rhetorical strategies and meta-task contributions. Especially for the latter competencies, I hope I have begun to contribute to a vocabulary of description that will allow students, instructors, researchers, and administrators to develop a baseline understanding of how multilingual English users can participate in and contribute to increasingly diverse composition courses. In addition, I hope I have identified research categories for further refinement and testing in first-year composition courses and beyond. In the face of the common assumption that multilingual users necessarily have limited experience with English-language contexts (Gibbons), I have attempted to demonstrate that they can and do negotiate successfully—if unexpectedly—and they draw on rhetorical and experiential knowledge to do so. Owing to their subtlety, identifying these competencies takes time for both students and instructors—time that is already tight in many composition curricula. Large questions remain about how to operationalize, assess, and even teach such competencies for the benefit of all English users. However, the possible payoff of augmenting composition teaching with a grounded, empirical approach is great. In the final two chapters, I discuss a pedagogical experiment to foreground these competencies, and I address important pedagogical questions in articulating a broad definition of composition as an architectonic for cultural and linguistic uncertainty.

NOTES

1. Genre theorists often turn to Bakhtin's statement that "genres must be fully mastered in order to be manipulated freely" (80). There is tension about this in Bakhtin, though, because Bakhtin is also clear that there is no way to create a list of available speech genres. Therefore, there is no way—before the enactment of genres in performance—to define mastery. Mastery is defined by users themselves in negotiating emerging contexts that call for particular genres.

2. In 1992, Glaser published *Basics of Grounded Theory Analysis: Emergence vs. Forcing*, in which he argued that his former partner, Anselm Strauss, and Strauss's student, Juliet Corbin, fundamentally misunderstood his approach. For Glaser, Strauss and Corbin had distorted the original grounded theory work—and its emphasis on the emergence of theoretical categories from data—in favor of an approach that "forced" categories into preconceived theories. At several points in his strongly polemical short book, Glaser accuses the two of plagiarizing the original work, and he asserts a legal claim for intellectual property.

3. Canagarajah, "Interrogating," "Negotiating"; Cook, "Competence"; Flowerdew; Harklau; Ibrahim; Kramsch and Lam; Land and Whitley; Leki, "Coping"; Lu, "Essay," "Professing"; Matsuda and Silva; Medgyes; Rampton; Widdowson.

4. At each university, I obtained local Institutional Review Board approval for my observations and interviews. I distributed general descriptions of my research as well as informed consent forms to all students and instructors present in each class on days I prescheduled. With the exception of the course I actually taught (described in Chapter 3), I solicited students' consent after asking their instructors to leave the classroom—a step deemed necessary by each review board to help avoid making students feel coerced to consent under the gaze of their teachers.

In my own class, I asked a colleague to distribute consent forms and to keep them in a location unknown to me until the end of the semester. The consent forms asked for students' and instructors' printed names and signatures as well as for a brief statement of what they considered to be their native language. Once I determined that consenting students in a class represented a combination of native-speaking and non-native-speaking English users, I scheduled observation days with the instructor that coincided with group tasks (especially peer review sessions for major writing assignments). In cases in which not all members of a given peer group had consented to participate in my research, I did not observe, record, or take notes on that group's activities. And I made every effort to stay out of audio-recording distance from other groups that included nonconsenting students.

5. Other emergent categories include "ethnographic observational skill," "leveraging expectations (of multilingual students' behavior)," "distancing (especially from native-speaking teachers)," "leveraging linguistic instincts," "leveraging oral experience," "rhetorical flexibility," "access to diverse contexts," and "empathy."

6. This name and all other participant names are pseudonyms.

7. This is the only course I have observed so far that was not a for-credit composition course. I decided to schedule observations and interviews for this class because of my familiarity with this instructor's basic writing syllabus, which is comparable to many sections of the for-credit first-year course.

8. Melanie's behavior appeared to parallel that of several participants in Leki's study, who "spoke of attempting to manipulate the cognitive demands of writing for their disciplinary courses by, for example, deferring attention to grammatical issues until they had generated the ideas in their texts to their own satisfaction" ("Coping" 253). Thus, in addition to a meta-task orientation, Melanie may also be exhibiting a sense of how to balance her own response competencies in the time allowed for response.

3

Composition: Outdated Assumptions to New Architectonics

> If the "wandering viewpoint" is a way to describe the way in which the reader is present in the text, then a reader with SWE [Standard Written English] expectations continues to wander rather aimlessly in a text by an ESL writer because the reader cannot recognize the signposts left by the writer. . . . Readers should allow themselves to be lost for a while, for readers who suspend judgment and thus become accustomed to recognizing a wider variety of rhetorical modes, will begin to alter their expectations, to widen them, a process which will ultimately permit them to interact with more types of texts, thereby enriching their reading processes.
>
> —Robert Land and Catherine Whitley

> But my counterpart does her research in Korean!
> —Student in ENGL 015, section 64,
> Penn State University, fall semester 2004

DURING ROUGHLY THE FIRST THIRD OF the experimentally linked mainstream–multilingual composition course I helped pilot at Penn State in fall 2004, my students—all but two of whom were native speakers of English from Pennsylvania and other parts of the Middle Atlantic—seemed on board with the idea of linguistic diversity. Many had traveled abroad themselves on family vacations, spring break or summer trips, or foreign language class field trips. Others had hosted foreign exchange students. Several had worked in restaurants in which they needed to learn at least a little Spanish in order to communicate with the rest of the staff. In addition, although they didn't say or write as much directly, they—like many Americans at this point—were immersed in multiple contexts that communicated "multiculturalism." They watched television commercials that used examples of African American Vernacular English to sell a variety of products (especially to high school– and college-age consumers), they were taking classes with teaching assistants who were from a variety of foreign countries and who spoke English with accents, and their composition instructor was asking them to write about their experiences with language learning. They seemed genuinely interested and engaged. They wrote interesting and even compelling "language-learning narratives," and they willingly participated in face-to-face and online conversations with their counterparts in a multilingual composition course.

All of this enthusiasm lasted right up to the point at which I reminded them that not only would they be reading and commenting on their multilingual counterparts' drafts, but that their counterparts would be reading *theirs* as well—that is, they would all be critiquing drafts of papers that would come in for me to grade. I responded to their anxious questions by reminding them about the discoveries they had already made through their experiences outside of class, through our course readings, and through their interactions with their counterparts: they were seeing clear evidence that English language learners, despite the labels attached to them, had skills using English in settings with higher stakes than even their composition course. This seemed fine in theory, but the rubber was hitting the road: they were working through their first semester at Penn State, and they were no doubt doing calculations about grades and time. As I wrote in my teaching journal about this time, a transition seemed to be occurring from "What's most interesting?" to "How much do I need to do?" Getting interesting and potentially useful comments from multilingual counterparts was, at this point, less of a priority than efficiently writing successful assignments for me to evaluate. Not that I blamed them. After all, they had two very powerful allies. The university had clearly sent them the message that they needed to learn as much about writing in fifteen weeks as they could to achieve success in upper-division courses (thus perpetuating the long-standing view of composition as necessary but ancillary). And their multilingual counterparts sometimes showed a lack of confidence in their ability to critique writing (thus giving fuel to arguments against peer review in L2-specific or "mixed" courses).

Such an experiment may not seem like an auspicious example of composition for the multilingual present and future. But despite the false starts and uncertainty both students and teachers faced in the piloted courses, promising possibilities emerged. In fact, to the extent that composition can be useful as a testing ground for ambiguities about increasing cultural and linguistic diversity, this experiment—which exposed limits to popular multicultural pedagogy and highlighted the difficulty of enacting more interactive "critical language awareness" (Gilyard, "Basic")—was a good first attempt to "debug." To take full advantage of the increasing presence of multilingual users in mainstream composition for the sake of those students, their native-English-speaking peers, and their teachers, composition needs to reorient to what the presence of multilingual users represents. The truncated practice of "comp" can grow into *composition* by expanding the scope of the act of composing: from efficient, conventionally acceptable texts into relationships and strategies that are essential to intercultural and linguistic negotiations. While this shift doubtless introduces considerable messiness and requires expanded time to do "word work" well (Lu, "Composition's"), I hope I have already begun to show that there is solid theoretical support for it. My own growing empirical research suggests its productivity, as well.

This chapter draws on rhetoric, literacy studies, and theories of foreign language teaching to present an expanded theoretical and pedagogical definition of the practice of composition in US colleges and universities in response to many of the conditions I have already outlined. It also presents a triangulated account of a piloted, cross-cultural composition course, which uncovers successes and failures.

COMPOSITION AND MAKING DESIGNS AVAILABLE

Perhaps the best statements about how composition can address twenty-first-century uncertainty appear in the work of twentieth-century rhetorician Kenneth Burke—especially in the context of Burke's productive interchange with his era's linguistics. Burke's articulation of rhetoric as a necessary and necessarily messy human condition encouraged sociolinguists like Dell Hymes to attend to actual *communities* as units of study rather than to abstract linguistic models. The work of Hymes and others has, as I noted, substantially influenced later approaches to foreign language and composition teaching. But Burke's own writings about pedagogy, I believe, may also be directly influential in reorienting composition, especially as his views mesh with more contemporary perspectives on design and on intercultural communicative competence.

Burke's preoccupation with disorderly human communities is understandable given the situations to which he was responding. Initially a literary critic and expounder of psychological, form-based approaches to literature, Burke turned his attention in the 1930s toward large-scale social changes that coincided with the Great Depression and the interwar period. He saw many economic problems as an effect of humans' typically competitive impulses. Humans' tendency—unique among living things—to respond to symbols and to crave associations with others meant that rhetorical identifications with people, causes, nations are inevitable. At times, such associations can produce positive results, but they can also (perhaps inevitably) turn destructive, and Burke saw warfare as the logical result of competition through symbols. His suggestion then was to use humanity's love of symbols to forestall its indulgence in unhealthy symbolic associations. If everyday associations were as rich with symbolic action as literary works, Burke believed, symbolic analysis could then be directly useful outside of literary texts. As an alternative to social orientations that caused people to ally on one side or another of issues of the day, and thus to ally against one another competitively, Burke proposed what he variously called a "comic" or "poetic" perspective that would seek to understand the rhetorical bases and limits of all social orientations:

Beginning with such a word as *composition* to designate the architectonic nature of either a poem, a social construct, or a method of practical action, we can take over the whole vocabulary of tropes (as formulated by the rhetoricians) to describe the specific patterns of human behavior. Since social life, like art, is a *problem of appeal*, the poetic metaphor would give us invaluable hints for describing modes of practical action which are too often measured by simple tests of utility and too seldom with reference to the communicative, sympathetic, *propitiatory* factors that are clearly present in the procedures of formal art and must be as truly present in those informal arts of living we do not happen to call arts. (*Permanence* 264)

It is unclear from this brief passage whether Burke intended *composition* to point to the university course. It is clear, however, from his other writings that Burke had designs for education that were relevant to fostering a poetic perspective.[1] He lays the foundations of a rhetorical pedagogy in his 1955 essay "Linguistic Approaches to Problems of Education." Burke begins by redefining humans as "the typically language-using, or symbol-using, animal," and he reiterates that approaches to human actions must recognize humans' condition as *linguistic* and not just biological. Education, then, must be based on theories that do not reduce human tendencies to behavioristic impulses. Problems appear when education gives in readily to individuals' competitive impulses: "The serious student enters school hoping to increase his powers, to equip himself in the competition for 'success,' to make the 'contracts' that get him a better-paying job." The supposed benefits of this pedagogy are not only individual. Burke argues that empires and nations benefit from instilling and encouraging competitive impulses, which tend to promote the business of war: "[A]lthough there is conceivable an ideal world of nationalisms that would be related to one another as peacefully as the varied portraits in an art gallery, we need no very difficult fables to admonish us about the ever-ready dialectical resource whereby national 'differences' may become national 'conflicts'" (271–72).

As an intervention, Burke advocates an educational program beyond teaching the refinement of competitive tendencies:

[O]ne hopes for ways whereby the various voices, in mutually correcting one another, will lead toward a position better than any one singly. That is, one does not merely want to outwit the opponent, or to study him, one wants to be affected by him, in some degree to incorporate him, to so act that his ways can help perfect one's own—in brief, to learn from him. ("Linguistic" 284)

In place of competition, students should learn "techniques for doubting much that is now accepted as lying beyond the shadow of a doubt" (272). Certainty for Burke is not a function of a given perspective's durability: it is instead a function of how often people who hold that perspective forget that *all* perspectives are rhetorical and limited. The key to getting around certainty, then, is employing a generally poetic, dramatistic, linguistic analysis. As Jessica Enoch puts it, "students are to immerse themselves in the various sides of the debate to learn how each side is made and remade through linguistic choices" (282). Thus, Burke's own rhetorical situation, populated as it was by world wars and a global depression, meant that he intended his pedagogy to be a brake on rhetorical and material competitiveness.

While Burke's focus on developing an analytic attitude to forestall war reflects a different preoccupation from that of other theorists I have been discussing, his embrace of the pedagogical value of slowing down parallels similar comments made by bell hooks, Min-Zhan Lu, and others. Inefficiency—at least compared to the more technical or capitalistic pedagogies he critiques—is at the heart of Burke's suggested program: "Education must be thought of as a *technique of preparatory withdrawal*, the institutionalizing of an attitude that one should be able to *recover at crucial moments*, all along the subsequent way" ("Linguistic" 273, emphasis in original). Inefficiency, patience, and comfort with ambiguity are also at the heart of contemporary efforts to refigure the presence and role of diverse English users. Even though Burke does not specifically address global evolutions in English, he makes a relevant point: "institutionalizing" an analytic attitude about symbol using—stepping to one side to gain the perspective that all groups and individuals draw from the same human symbolic resources—"would sharpen our sense of the fact that all men, as symbol-users, are of the same substance, in contrast with naïve views that in effect think of aliens as of a different substance" (286). Burke makes a strong statement about efforts to compete with individuals and groups that appear separated by cultural and national boundaries. While competition may serve some national end, it does not ultimately serve humanistic ends. Where English-language pedagogies have historically attempted to eradicate, modify, ignore, or simply tolerate "alien" differences, Burke would have pedagogy open the question of whether those differences represent symbolic resources.

Perhaps the most integrated recent attempt to open language pedagogy to such resources appears in the design-oriented literacy work of the New London Group (Cope and Kalantzis) and of Richard Kern.[2] Drawing on M. A. K. Halliday's articulation of "language as social semiotic," these researchers postulate that language always responds to particular social conditions and always exploits local conditions. This line of argument is similar to that of other new literacy studies theorists (Gee; Street) who discuss "Discourses" as virtual communities that have their own rules for effective communication. But the design-oriented theorists go further toward laying out a complete pedagogy. Effective communication, in their view, depends on carrying out communicative goals with an eye toward the resources available to support those goals. The interaction of goals and resources often builds a bridge between previously available resources and new resources that appear when literate individuals rework the material they have. In these theorists' terms, language users access "Available Designs," use those designs in "Designing" (interpreting and/or producing texts), and then create reproductive or transformative texts that provide "Re-Designed" resources for their own or others' future use, thus giving rise to newly "Available Designs."

Taking a design-oriented approach seriously—especially in diverse settings such as composition courses—means paying attention to the possibility that some Available Designs might not be immediately recognizable as legitimate resources for either English language learners or their native-English-speaking peers and teachers, who are usually considered the "experts" in English-language contexts. While Burke ("Linguistic") suggests that "alien" symbolic resources are theoretically at par with "domestic" ones, making such designs actually Available might require significant scaffolding. There is considerable room in the Design sequence for operationalizing the kinds of competencies that have emerged in my research—for injecting "alien" Designs into the Designing cycle. For instance, Kern mentions but does not provide examples of experimental syntax, but the lexical and syntactic innovations that appear in Widdowson and Lu ("Professing") seem appropriate. And since peer collaboration on writing assignments continues to be a popular feature of composition courses, the pragmatic strategies that certain multilingual English users have employed (in my observations) to move tasks along and maintain group dynamics could be read as valuable Designs. Thinking broadly beyond linguistic and classroom considerations, there is certainly utility in expanding *topoi* through intercultural and international interactions, as several students I have observed did—especially in yet another era of international and intercultural conflict.

FROM AWARENESS TO APPLICATION

I come full circle here to the experimental cross-cultural composition course I helped pilot, because these idealistic and practical arguments were precisely the ones I was making to students enrolled in that course. As I mentioned, they were on board with them for the most part, and many of them wrote about intercultural and interlinguistic interactions they had had in uncertain situations. They had been both language experts and novices themselves, so they had had opportunities to play the usual role of the language learner struggling with a sense of her or his own symbolic competencies. But the transition between their past experiences—often in higher-stakes contexts than their composition course—and their current experiences working with diverse peers in analyzing and writing texts was uneven. In this section, I describe the piloted course in more detail and provide analyses of several sources of data from the course. By presenting portions of students' face-to-face and computer-mediated interactions, course assignments, peer review comments, and my own teaching journal, I hope to present a triangulated view of what happened when theories about the value of negotiating cultural and linguistic uncertainty translated to pedagogical goals in a first-year composition course. As I relate, there were both successes and failures. But my own advocacy for such a pedagogy is undiminished: the problems I note uncover opportunities for further refinement.[3]

Challenges arose early: even though my co-teacher, Susan Bobb, and I met regularly before and during the course and worked well together, it was difficult to overcome the cultural differences (Atkinson and Ramanathan) between the courses. My section, as part of the Department of English's Composition Program, focused on rhetorical approaches to composing texts for a variety of audiences in and out of the university. Susan's section, as part of the Department of Linguistics and Applied Language Studies' second language composition sequence, focused largely on writing research-based arguments for academic audiences. In addition, students in my section were required to complete six major writing assignments, whereas Susan's would complete three. These content- and scheduling-based differences posed a challenge for integrating material and teaching: even though we had planned for students' assignments across sections to dovetail and had even discussed the possibility of trading teaching with each other, we were unable to integrate our courses beyond some readings, conversational activities, and occasional peer review sessions.

Despite these obstacles, students' interactions produced valuable data that fill in more of the picture I began to draw in Chapter 2. As I read and report on these data, I continue the grounded analysis I undertook in that chapter.[4] In the linked, intercultural course, I observed more instances of the multilingual competencies I had noted in my regular course. I also observed members of my mainstream section deploying their own intercultural strategies and refining them through writing assignments and online and face-to-face interactions with their counterparts in the second language section. These students' awareness and articulation of strategies in this course is a good sign that future courses can leverage the linguistic and rhetorical knowledge students bring with them—even students who, on the surface, do not appear to have had much experience with diversity before entering the university.

"I CAN ACTUALLY UNDERSTAND WHAT HE WANTS!" ATTITUDES AND NEGOTIATIONS

Early in the semester, I tried to establish a kind of baseline for students to reflect on their previous experiences with linguistic diversity before they encountered their multilingual counterparts. In their first assignment—a language-learning narrative—students described a wide range of situations in which they had to interact with language learners or negotiate contexts as language learners themselves. What emerged from their writing were consistent comments about the difficulty of language learning and about the need to develop relevant attitudes and abilities. Several wrote about experiences during summer or part-time jobs in restaurants and amusement parks. Others described hosting exchange students or befriending international students in their high schools. A couple recalled experiences traveling, specifically to Italy and Québec, in which the Italian and French they had taken in their classes at home did not match the language they were hearing in host family conversations, in restaurants, and in markets. Clear from many students is the sense that, regardless of how it is done, learning languages takes significant time and attention and that the effort involved should prompt language "experts" to be empathetic. Students who wrote about their time in high school foreign language classrooms were especially direct:[5]

> One thing I have realized about learning is that you need to be involved in what you're doing, as well as do extra work. I took four years of Spanish class in high school, each year rising a level in difficulty. The difficulty was just the beginning

though. Every year, the teacher would throw a million new vocabulary words at you, all of which were to be memorized and used. A new personal story, of a few Spanish-speaking people, was told from the textbook every year as well, and on top of that, even more verbs and their rules or uses were presented. Not that it wasn't important to learning the language; it just made it more challenging to take in so much information at once.

Another student described her high school French class similarly and went on to write about her frustration during a class trip in encountering Québecois who were not willing to wait for her to try her French, "especially when you are trying as hard as possible to speak properly."

Students commonly responded to their sensitivities about language learning by attempting positive attitudes and reciprocation. Probably half of the students echoed one writer's remark that patience is the most important attitude and that the use of a kind of intercultural golden rule is key to overcoming at least the possibility of bad feelings: "Imagine if the situation were reversed, one would want the same done for them." One student who traveled to Italy related an "epiphany" in which she realized the value of language not as a communicative medium but as a way to express respect: "By speaking a few Italian words I would show [shopkeepers] I was attempting to learn about their culture: about who they were and about the place I was visiting." Several other students recalled working in family-owned Mexican restaurants and trying to surmount language barriers with recently immigrated and largely monolingual Spanish-speaking staffers. In those situations, there is often time for casual interactions, but the stakes involved in misunderstanding can often be high for servers, managers, and customers:

Occasionally I would say hi to [Daisy], but now I had to actually communicate a problem to her. I had to make sure she understood me so the customer would not yell at me and tell my manager. Fortunately it was slow that day, so I wasn't under a lot of pressure to quickly fix the problem. I began by communicating the situation in English. "You forgot the chicken, can you add it?" Daisy understood the word "chicken" and pointed to it to make sure that it was what I was talking about. When I confirmed it with a smile, she immediately added the chicken to the salad and the problem was solved.

In this case, the student and her costaff member were able to take advantage of the time they had to clarify, and the student was able to wear away at the potential barrier between herself and Daisy by demonstrating a positive attitude, one that—in the student's view—led to further positive interactions.

Beyond their reflections about attitudes, students wrote of specific strategies that showed their attempts to take advantage of the resources at hand. Gestures and other nonverbals were the most commonly reported strategies, and they seemed to be especially prominent in the context of physical activities prevalent in high schools. Several students took ballet and other forms of dance with international instructors, at least some of whom were not (at least, to the students' ears) fluent in English. One student remembered having one Cuban and two Russian teachers with whom she needed to negotiate nonverbal strategies for conveying counts, steps, and the like:

[Roberto, her teacher] could not find the right words in English so he would simply say the ballet term for the part of the combination that needed fixed. Well, I could understand what step was incorrect but not why. This was extremely frustrating not only for me but for him as well. Roberto's body was to old to demonstrate the steps effectively. He simply could not make his muscles move the way they needed to. So here we are staring at each other, language differences sitting between us. For weeks this went on to no avail. . . . Then, like a light went off in his head, he did the step exaggerating the mistake I was making. "Thank God!" I thought, "I can actually understand what he wants."

Students also reported their use of strategies that more closely resemble the emerging competencies I observed in Chapter 2. Several discussed using what I might call ethnographic methods, including triangulation and consulting cultural informants. The dancer quoted earlier emphasized the extent to which she was closely observing both linguistic attempts and paralinguistic strategies like gestures commonly used in dance programs. To understand one of her Russian teachers, the student remembered collaborating with fellow dancers in watching the teacher's movements. Eventually, they realized the teacher was using a dance syllabus she assumed the students were also using. The two students who traveled to Italy for study and vacations recalled letting local shoppers go ahead of them in city markets so they could watch them negotiate prices. One student wrote about her first time using online chat in terms that mirror others' recollections of entering foreign language contexts:

> I entered my first chat room, and the members were using abbreviations like "LOL" and "BRB." I had no idea what these or any of the other short hand stood for. I sat back for about 5 minutes, taking all of the conversation from the chat room in. After that, I was becoming quite frustrated because I wanted to participate, but didn't know what they were saying.
>
> I instant messaged one of the people in the chat room, asking them if they could help me out with the lingo. Luckily they were really friendly about it, and told me what a lot of the abbreviations meant. I put their screen name on my buddy list and I would ask them any questions I had as time went on about the chat room talk.

I was pleased by the extent to which students could recall and articulate their preuniversity language-learning and negotiating strategies, and I wanted to encourage them to develop and refine them. In my comments on their reading responses and narratives, I asked pointed questions about managing cultural and linguistic diversity, and I scaffolded possible responses in keeping with my goals for the course. Most of my comments emphasized the typical tendency to place the communicative burden solely on the learner, and they highlighted challenges to that tendency. In response to the ballet student's writing—that her Cuban teacher had to exaggerate the mistake she was making in order to be understood—I wrote,

"It's usually the other way around—the *language learner* makes the mistake and the native speaker corrects it" (emphasis in original). I praised another student's expressed realization that her neighbor, a Spaniard, was probably more frustrated with trying to communicate than her English-speaking friends: "You seem to recognize here that the burden can't rest with one person *alone. Both* people have to find creative ways around." In other comments, I attempted to make connections between what students were remembering and intercultural skills they would need to develop in our class and beyond. One student related how her knowledge of Spanish–English cognates helped her determine that someone needed medical attention. I wrote:

> You're describing an experience with working in-between languages in order to do something that neither English nor Spanish could do alone. Lots of people learning English in the US have to do this every day as they move from family to school to work, etc. It's a skill that will become more important.

Susan, my co-teacher, scaffolded similar responses, reflecting, I believe, a successful attempt to integrate our strategies. In one comment she shared with me from her responses to multilingual users' writing, she responded to a student's observation about the usefulness of scheduled conversations to improve spoken English: "While the conversations may help improve your English, the program was set up for *both* ESL and ENGL[ish] students to learn about communication" (emphasis in original). Another student recalled her conversation with counterparts in my class about author Maria Cunha's autobiographical account of acting as her father's interpreter when she was a child: "Our counterparts were not able to relate a whole lot to Cunha but [my classmate] and I were able to relate to her article a whole lot more than our counterparts." Susan replied, "My guess is that you and [your classmate] helped your ENGL counterparts a lot in understanding the article!"

At roughly the same time they were writing these assignments, my students met their counterparts in Susan's multilingual composition course. Before the meeting, Susan and I assigned students to eleven groups of varying size. The difference in the size of the two courses (eighteen in the linguistics course and twenty-four in English) meant that all groups would not be of equal size. To compensate and to ensure participation, Susan and I attempted to group the more vocal students from both classes together and separate them from students from both classes who, we felt, might have been overpowered. To break the ice, we asked each group to address several questions:

1. Why did you come to Penn State?
2. What do you plan to study?
3. What was your learning experience like in high school, and what was a typical day like?
4. What are differences in the ways you use language with different people and in different situations?
5. What are your experiences with people who do not speak your native language?

We assigned each group a digital voice recorder and microphone. Because all of the groups were meeting in the same classroom (we lacked nearby classrooms to use to split the large group), the quality of the recordings from small groups varied considerably: at times, noise from the conversations overwhelmed the recording capacity of the microphones.

However, audio recordings and students' written summations of the conversations were rich enough to show that students in both classes quickly learned about one another. They discovered that their counterparts were not quite what they expected, although that meant very different things for different groups. There were clear differences from group to group, for instance, in the extent to which Susan's students participated in guiding the conversations along. A few students seemed intent on answering the questions I posed in order, and they invited participation from each of the other group members. In other groups, students from my section directed questions and conversations. Topics ranged from interna-

tional travel to the sizes of high school graduating classes to sports. The whole range of topics revealed significant diversity among the students who were collectively labeled ESL. Several students in my section wrote of their group members that they were interested, relieved, and surprised to find many similarities. "Our whole group are in majors that have math as a strong focus," one student wrote. She went on to note that "[w]e have all also known that Penn State was the college we wanted to attend for quite some time." Another student recalled his group's discussion of similarities between school systems in locations as diverse as Germany, Saudi Arabia, and the United States, and he recalled his own surprise that the Saudi student had studied English as extensively as he had.[6] A Kuwaiti student in another group related his extensive English-learning experience in a British-style high school in his home country. But other students were equally surprised by extensive cultural differences:

> I was apauled [sic] to find out that in South Korea the students attend school from 8am to 11pm. Both of my counterparts, from South Korea and Haiti, said all they do is sleep, go to school, and do work. They both seem happy to be here in the US, although they seem scared. I never really realized how different other countries are from the US. . . . I feel like I have been sheltered/naïve about those cultural differences.

Whereas the impression this student's counterparts gave was of foreign school systems that were more rigorous than in the United States, another group discussed schools abroad that were more lax:

> I also learned that school is not taken as seriously in Puerto Rico as it is here. They could not go to school or not attend class and it wouldn't be such a big deal. Here, if you did that in high school, you would have plenty of work to make up when you got back and if you were caught skipping class, you were promptly given a Saturday school or a suspension.

Frequently, conversations in groups turned to attempts to find common ground despite often significant differences in culture, language, and educational background. In their written summations of these conversations, students in my section alluded to the effect of these attempts: increasing comfort levels for many groups despite initially feeling "thrown together," in one student's words. Chosen majors were a popular topic. Penn State is a well-known engineering school, and it recruits international students at undergraduate and graduate levels for its engineering programs, so several students across groups shared a desire to work their way into related majors. And where majors were widely different and did not give rise to much conversation, students actively sought out common experiences. Three of the four students in one group seemed perplexed about why their counterparts came to Penn State: the US students came because they grew up following Penn State athletics and—for one—because he was specifically interested in majoring in golf management. One of the international multilingual users came to Penn State because he was already employed by a major Saudi oil company, which was paying for his tuition and other expenses. Fairly abruptly, one of the US students asked, "Did you guys watch the [2004] Olympics at all?" For several minutes after that, the conversation centered on basketball—a sport in which the United States and Germany (the home country of the other multilingual user in the group) had done comparatively well. The conversation then led to a brief discussion of the German student's plan to return home to join his country's soccer team for the 2008 Olympics. Another group consisted of students from both sections who were from very different locations but who were able to "bond over sibling responsibilities and arguments" since they were both the oldest sisters in their families. Much of this initial conversation, then, was off-topic compared to the questions I asked them to address and compared to the narrative they had read. However, what emerged from the activity was a clear picture of students who, despite preclassroom differences, shared the experience of entering a major US university—a transition as challenging for these diverse students as for the adult students in Roz Ivanič's study. What also emerged was students' desire on both sides to try to learn more about their differences and similarities and become more comfortable in their interactions.

MIXING COMPETENCIES AND
RESPONDING RHETORICALLY

I was encouraged by students' reactions to this early conversation, especially their attempts to find commonalities when none may have initially appeared during their often awkward introductions. I was particularly interested in the possibility that these attempts to identify with one another might prove useful for later activities that would require them to respond to one another's work rhetorically. I wondered, for example, how their fairly general conversations would translate to specific work on assignment-based invention and drafting.

Once we decided to shift to peer review in assigned cross-class groups, we also decided to ask students to do their peer work online. Our decision was informed by several factors. First, we wanted to address the difficulty students were having coordinating out-of-class, face-to-face meetings, and we believed that allowing students to work online would give them a way around that problem. Second, we believed it would encourage students to integrate writing more closely into their interactions, since there was no way for them to interact online *without* writing. In addition, I was intrigued by possibilities that online peer review offered that face-to-face work might not. Several scholars (Hansen and Liu; Pennington) have observed multilingual users' increased motivation in online settings compared to traditional print. Anecdotally, I had observed numerous international students using chat and other online utilities to communicate with friends and family in their home countries and as a way around international long-distance rates. Thus, I saw the chance to leverage students' existing experience with computer-mediated communication into relatively high-stakes interactions with their peers.

Despite some initial technical difficulties, most students in both sections successfully used online tools to share responses to drafts and to brainstorming notes.[7] Students drew on some of the interactional skills they displayed in their conversations, but they added new ones that seemed well suited to both the medium and the assignments. My own teaching journal entry from just after the computer lab meeting provides an overview of concepts and themes that were already emerging:

1. Prioritizing error correction: 2 of my students asked how they should address the issue of grammatical unfamiliarities in a draft in which there appear to be a lot of them. They said they felt they had time because of the shortness of the draft to go back and at least try some close editing-type commenting after they had done the "higher-level" commenting I've reminded them to do. They presented the solution, themselves, of finding the most pressing or most prevalent ones—the ones that most impeded their understanding—and addressing those. My response was that that's basically what teachers do.

2. Getting over the confidence problem: Susan reports that one of her students asked if it was OK for my students to use "I" in their writing. She said basically, "ask that on the Wiki." We took the fact that he asked as a good sign of confidence in giving comments to a "native speaker."

3. Comments vs. direct editing: I haven't counted yet, but I see that a number of students decided to comment using the built-in Wiki "comment" utility rather than writing their comments on the drafts, themselves. I'm not sure what that means yet.

4. The "seventh-grade dance" effect: They've met for conversations, but they automatically split into [separate] classes when they came into the lab—Susan's students in the back, mine in the front.

5. Keeping it in the family: Initially, it really appeared that my students were commenting on other ENGL students and the ESL students were keeping to themselves. Eventually, they branched out. A couple of students asked what they should do after they had read "their one draft," but many just went on and found someone else to comment on.

Even this early computer-mediated work showed evidence of students in both sections retooling conversational strategies to make them work in this interactive but definitely *nonconversational* medium. For instance, since the wiki did not allow for synchronous communication (such as chat or instant messaging), students were unable to attempt immediate repairs of misunderstandings by using gesture or other paralinguistic strategies, by developing lingua francas, or by circumlocuting until they found words that best fit the context. For several students in my section, this meant prioritizing response—attempting to determine rhetorical context and purpose from the writing they saw and using that to gauge which mechanical issues were most relevant. For Susan and me, students' initial patterns of wiki use, especially their tendency to comment on drafts from their own sections only, prompted more scaffolding to ensure cross-class interactions.

By the end of the meeting in the computer lab, students were branching out to respond to others' drafts. In reporting on students' responses, I focus particular attention on the strategies second language users employed in commenting on their native-English-speaking counterparts' work. Some students couched their comments—even on topics that did not overtly engage intercultural issues—in their own cultural experiences, much as several students did in mainstream sections I observed. One student responded to a counterpart's draft arguing for more support for art education in the United States that

> I am totally with you because there have been a lot of geniuses in field of music, art, architecture. All brilliant people we know are in field of art. The same problem has been happening in Korea, every single high school say that they really want to support art but they do not have money. I don't think it can be a reason that we ignore art courses. The priority should be given to the art courses.

But while I note similarities between this course and the mainstream courses I observed (see Chapter 2), students' use of the wiki—and the corresponding lack of fixed time constraints on their responses, unlike in the traditional sections of first-year composition—appeared to afford responses that mixed the competencies I listed in Chapter 2:

1. "Book" knowledge of English grammar
2. Lexical and syntactic innovation
3. Linguistic and/or rhetorical resistance/accommodation
4. Cross-cultural information/critique
5. Meta-task orientation
    a. Meta-discursive sensitivity
    b. Group dynamic sensitivity

For example, several students made meta-discursive suggestions about transitions, thesis statements, and cohesion along with critical notes about book-based grammar and style—all combined with information based on their position as cultural informants. Several students in my section wrote position papers or proposals about the SAT and other standardized tests.[8] One student drafted some initial research about the SAT's ability to predict college-level success, concluding that other factors are often just as important and that schools should consider dropping the test. In addition, she argued that businesses relied on altogether different criteria for hiring decisions and that colleges should align their practices with corporate ones:

> A study performed by DYG Inc, concluded that more than ninety percent of businesses and their employees rate character as the most important quality an individual could possess when entering the work world. . . . A standardized test score is meaningless in the workplace, and as a result, should not be considered as important with college admissions because college is supposed to prepare one for that workplace.

This student's multilingual counterpart agreed that college often prepares students for business but responded that differences matter: "[O]ne is for choosing students who have the ability of studying and the other does for choosing worker who 'will' help their company and do well for its growth." In addition, the multilingual user noted that US colleges and universities are not as insistent about standardized tests as her counterpart was picturing them, especially compared to international contexts:

I think the evaluation student shoul [sic] depend on the college itself. They might consider that SAT/ACT scores are more important or GPAs in high school are. And in U.S. it is more flexible than my country. (We have only one test, and it decides almost everything about me). Additionally, in my case (for international student), Pennstate did not require my SAT/ACT scores. (some other college do also).

Probably the clearest example of this mixing occurred in a native-Arabic-speaking student's response to his counterpart in the mainstream course who was writing about conceptions of terrorism. Not surprisingly, given the current cultural and political climate in the United States, the mainstream student—although questioning prevalent ideas about terrorists—equated them with Islam in a way his multilingual counterpart found questionable. Interestingly, comments that reveal the multilingual user's role as cultural informant appeared alongside meta-discursive commentary (Susan's student's comments appear in boldface):

Now would be a good time to state that I do not condone what terrorists are doing, nor am I asking you to believe in their cause. I just ask that you look at them just as you would look at your neighbor. **I liked the way you proposed your opinion.** Terrorist are people just like you and me. They have their own beliefs that differ from our own. They have their own religion, Islam. **Are all terrorists Muslims? I really doubt!** The true meaning of Islam is a commitment to live in peace through submission to the will of Allah (Islam) **Good paraphrasing.** In Islam politics are not separated from religion. **Maybe you need to link those two sentences** There is also no writing the Qur'an that commends terrorist actions. The Qur'an actual speaks out against terrorism when it says "Fight in the cause of God against those who fight you, but do not begin aggression, for god loves not aggressors."(Islam) **Maybe it will be better if you cite it as (Qur'an 2:190)** Islam is a peaceful religion that has been turned over by a few bad people. Because Muslims believe that the Qur'an is written with the words of Allah himself, they believe that they are required to be terrorists **I am not sure about how the Islamic believe that Qur'an is written with the worlds of Allah himself, would make them believe they should be terrorists.** The corrupt leaders are using writings from the Qur'an such as "And when ye meet those who disbelieve—then striking off their head until ye have massacred them all." (Johnson) The Qur'an also states that those slain in gods cause will enter paradise. Some Muslim leaders have taken these saying out of context and have been teaching people the words of Allah in which they believe to be true. **Nice, but can you show clearer what is the correct interpretation of this, make sure you search in Islamic websites**

During their conversations early in the semester, the two Arabic-speaking students in Susan's section mentioned to their counterparts in my class that they had taken extensive course work in English in their home countries, including some courses in composition. This student's experience was apparent in his comments about paraphrasing and sentence style. It was also apparent in his note that the student writer should cite the Qur'an properly—a comment that also showed the multilingual student's specific knowledge of that text. At the same time that he advised the student to use a correct citation, he also pushed him to present more specific and credible information about connections between Islamic beliefs and terrorist acts. Additionally, he reflected a balance in his commentary similar to the balance Melanie exhibited in Chapter 2. On a draft about terrorism and Islam, it might be easy to lose such a balance in response to a largely unwarranted connection between the two. However, positive comments (about the writer's introduction of his position and about his reading of incorrect Qur'anic interpretations) interweaved with critical ones. And critical comments were often phrased as questions or hedged.

In fact, several other second language users used similar hedging strategies in commenting on counterparts' drafts. Numerous commentators have taken multilingual English users' performance in peer review as evidence of uncertainty or discomfort (Allaei and Connor; Nelson and Carson; Zhang, "Reexamining," "Thoughts").

But read in the context of other competencies operating in their interactions with native-English-speaking counterparts, this hedging may be evidence of rhetorical competence—especially as it prompts native-English-speaking students' consideration of alternative viewpoints. In other words, hedging may perform a function similar to the cultural informant function I noted earlier and in Chapter 2. In one example, a multilingual user who was actually a member of my mainstream section commented on a paper arguing for foreign language teaching at earlier ages in the United States:

> As I read your paper, I did not see any "positives" on learning a second language at a later age. Is there any positives? Is the only reason a second language is taught a later age because it is tradition and we have to focus on English? I am interested in the writing, because I feel the same way and have experience in learning another language when I was young, English. How would you get an audience who do not really care for this subject more interested, I did see that it can help them later in life, but what if they already passed that point. Good paper overall, I enjoyed it and found it interesting. If you can add more facts to strengthen your point on learning a language when you are younger. I think I only read three major points, but that could just be me.

In this comment, the student combined relevant personal experience—his own language-learning background—with a suggestion about broadening the appeal to readers who may themselves be older. At the end of the comment, the student also suggested that more reasons and evidence be added in support of the student writer's central claim, but he hedged on the number of reasons the student writer provides and opened the possibility of a misunderstanding ("that could just be me"). In another group, one of the students from the mainstream section had drafted an argument in defense of Penn State's mid-fall study day or fall break, claiming that students needed the day off for a variety of purposes. The multilingual reviewer combined several kinds of comments with a hedge about her knowledge of the issue:

> I really like your topic, also I didn't know that they try to re-move "study day" from us. -_-;;.. (It's really good information for me.. thank you!!).. I think your essay is well-organized and flows well.. I agree with what Katie said about your paper that you adequately used two counterparts of argument to make balance. But it would be better if you make new paragraph and more mention about students who really need a study day for its "true intent." And I wish you would add more specific follow-up information about the debate. (Audiences who don't know much about this issue but are really inter-ested, just like me, would want to know what is really going on now..+o+)

While the student claimed little knowledge of the debate about the study day, she clearly demonstrated knowledge of meta-discursive vocabulary (about organization and flow) and also showed her en-gagement in the review task by referencing the other group mem-ber's (Katie's) comments. In this context, her hedging became a way to emphasize the student writer's need to "add more specific follow-up information" in order to make a clearer case for "interested" students, like her, who were unfamiliar with the issue.

In a third example, the multilingual user appeared to be familiar with the issue—in this case, the environmental impact of nuclear power plants—but disclaimed his comments about style and argu-ment support:

> I thought we are not supposed use words as I, you, we and such (first and second point of view?) in the writing.

> You probably should not refer your pesonal experience in a paper, the paper does not look unbiased when personal emo-tion is involved.

> I think you are focusing too much on the safety issues, you should talk more about other issues about nuclear plants, maybe how nuclear plants affect nearby communities.

> I thought your paper was very good. ther are a lot of informa-tion (may be too much) to support your argument.

Don't get upset by my comments.. hey what do i know? i am in ESL.

For the assignment the student writer was working on, I had asked students to research multiple sides of an issue of their choice and discuss how their position on the issue had evolved as a result of their work. Thus, I expected and even encouraged them to use personal language—at least, during their reflective statement near the end of their draft. Susan and I had given the multilingual users in her section copies of the assignment description that mentioned this element of the paper, so they should have been aware of it. However, Susan's section did not include a similar assignment, so the shift to personal language may have seemed strange. For this particular draft, however, the multilingual user appeared to respond to an especially stark shift from reporting research to reporting on personal opinion: at the end of the draft, the student shifted from citing a government report on new plant construction to a topic sentence in the final paragraph about how her opinion had not changed. Additionally, Susan's student proposed another line of argument beyond safety and critiqued the presence of "too much" information. Only after those comments does he end with the self-deprecating line, "hey what do i know? i am in ESL." Read in light of the assignment, which required students in my section to research several different perspectives, his suggestion to push for more diverse lines of argument was entirely appropriate. Couched as they were in his plea that the student writer should not "get upset" by his comments, the hedging about his ability to respond appeared to be more of an attempt to *increase* his comments' efficacy than to decrease it.

At the end of the semester, I asked students in my section to write about how well they believed the course had gone for them. Their writing about the goals most relevant to interacting with their multilingual counterparts continued to show their awareness of and sensitivity to the position of multilingual users and the challenges and opportunities they face and represent. Many themes that emerged in their writing early in the semester reappeared. A typical, general response connected the cross-course collaboration to real-world skills:

I already had an awareness and an open-mind to the ESL students here at Penn State. I didn't know they had special classes here for them though. By being in a course that involved collaboration with ESL students, I learned how they function in a big school, their obstacles, and their stories. The student my group worked with was really interesting, and I believe he helped my group understand that he's just another normal kid with the same problems like us. This interaction between Penn State ESL students and non-ESL students was one of the many that we will have to deal with when going out into the real world after college and beyond.

Several responses continued earlier themes of learning about the need to slow down and increase consciousness of slang and idiomatic expressions in oral, written, and online interactions. Students also replied that they needed to circumlocute—especially during conversations—in order to explain some terms to their counterparts. One student couched these kinds of comments in terms of her insight about the need to compromise:

> Before coming to Penn State I had limited experiences with ESL students. Most of my friends in high school . . . had[9] a good grasp on the English language as a result. However, the experiences I had with these friends hurt me more than it helped when it came time to interact with people who didn't speak English as well as I was used to it being spoken. The interactions with my ESL counterpart, as well as the interactions I have on a daily basis with my roommate (she was born in Hong Kong and English is not her native language), have made me realize that there will always need to be some compromise on my part to help someone who does not understand English as well as I do. There are two sides to a conversation and if one person is making an effort while the other person is not then the conversation will not benefit everyone.

But alongside these responses about their sensitivity, mainstream students also reacted to the pragmatic value of the course for their own linguistic and rhetorical practices going forward. One student wrote that, more than learning about the "diverse nature of Penn State," she learned about "how it is imperative to work through linguistic problems and/or uncertainties." Another student cited increased confidence in her ability to address misunderstandings in and out of class. Two other students felt an impact on their rhetorical choices. One noted that the "awareness" she gained through interactions with her counterparts prompted her to attempt to use "language that could be universally applied" so that her writing, albeit for specific audiences, would not discriminate on the basis of linguistic diversity. A second student was clear about the role cross-course peer review in particular played in her writing strategies:

> By sharing some of our papers with our ESL counterparts, and taking their criticism into account, I believe I adjusted some of my papers to expand to a more diverse audience. This was a direction I had never done before, and I found it interesting to write a paper more towards the general public rather than just a specific group.

I was pleased that the combined courses prompted students to take new directions in their writing and language learning. My own interactions with students in both sections taught me that they certainly had "done" this direction before, but they had not been asked to do it as a legitimate educational activity. They had not seen the value of negotiating differences for their own learning as users of language and rhetoric.

CONCLUSION

At the end of the semester in which we co-taught the piloted course, Susan and I met to discuss our own reactions. Students generally felt positive about the course, but many in both sections suggested that we include more opportunities for them to interact, especially for purposes of peer review. When they said this during class meetings, both Susan and I shrugged our response: we would have liked to, but the sections were too dissimilar. We did discuss possible compromises, such as meeting in the middle on the numbers of major assignments in order to expand time for interaction and revision. But the more I thought about time, the more I realized that the skills we were asking students to develop would require more time than we could ever allow in this or any single course. As a researcher, I appreciate that the categories emerging from the piloted course and from my observations in other courses give rise to further research that I can take time to do: analyzing interactions in more (and different) settings to confirm the emerging categories and operationalizing these categories as new Available Designs for pedagogical and policy purposes. As a composition teacher, I see these emerging categories and competencies fitting to some extent into existing pedagogical programs. Frequently, instructors and programs assess students on the basis of effective revision, so they could be responsive to the argument that students revise when they interact with peers who bring different cultural and rhetorical perspectives, as the students in my course did. But revision in the course may not be the only or even most appropriate gauge of such a course's intercultural work. How can compositionists best balance the work that *can* be done in their courses with the work that *should* be done to flesh out composition as a necessarily intercultural practice? In the final chapter, I suggest pedagogical directions for achieving this balance and for situating composition in contexts of increasingly complex relationships—rich grounds for the work that the students I have already observed are prepared for and excited about.

NOTES

1. Burke is perhaps best known to compositionists for his articulation of the *pentad,* an analytic frame that he proposes as part of his overall metaphor of "dramatism." Burke believed that if social relations can be read symbolically, it was desirable to create a "grammar of motives" (laid out in his well-known book of the same title) with which situations could effectively be "read" as acts in an unfolding human drama. Questions about *act, scene, agent, agency,* and *purpose* could guide determinations of who was acting, why, through what means, and in response to what conditions. In addition, these questions could be considered in "ratios" with one another so that the effects of, for instance, a given scene on the acts of actors in that scene would be revealed. Of course, it is easy to reduce this collection of questions to a prescriptive pedagogical guide,

and Ellen Quandahl argues that that does happen in composition teaching. Citing one example, Quandahl notes a tendency to teach the pentad as an aid to inventing new arguments rather than as a way to analyze situations *prior to* or even instead of entering the fray : "Such work . . . necessitates an understanding of how identity is culturally formed, of the identifications and conflicts present in human interaction. More than anything, Burke teaches ways to track the terms of such identifications and conflicts textually, and that work is central to his own writing and to the program of education that he proposes" (17). Burke makes the same point more directly in "Questions and Answers about the Pentad": "Aristotle's list [of topics] is telling the writer what to *say*, but the pentad is in effect telling the writer what to *ask*" (332, emphasis in original).

2. This literacy-based view of design contrasts with more literal connections between rhetoric and the fields of product design and architecture (see Kaufer and Butler).

3. The course I piloted is not a new concept. Several other attempts to teach cross-cultural composition have been made. Purdue University offers perhaps the best-known cross-cultural option. Begun in 1993, the course is scheduled alongside mainstream and multilingual composition sections. Since the course started, most, if not all, of the native-English-speaking students have come from Purdue's Department of Management, which has allowed the course instructors to control the mix of monolingual native-speaking and multilingual backgrounds. Although assignments have changed over ensuing years, the general pattern of work in the course has consistently stressed high levels of interaction through purposefully mixed small groups, in-class interviews and exploratory writing about cultural comparisons, and research-based writing about language diversity. Later instantiations of the course have bolstered ethnographic research elements: the nonverbal communication assignment that Nathan and Stephanie were collaborating on (described in Chapter 2) is an example of students' observational activities. The course has also required students to complete portfolios showing their writing progress as well as reflections on their cross-cultural experiences.

I drew on Purdue's example to structure the course I planned to pilot, but the institutional differences between Purdue and Penn State, as well as my own preferences, prompted me to make two key modifications:

> **Separate, rather than integrated, classes.** Purdue's Department of English includes faculty and graduate students in rhetoric and composition, English as a second language, and linguistics. This makeup allows for significant collaboration between instructors

in different departmental strands, and it also produces faculty and graduate instructors who are trained in both mainstream and multilingual composition. Given the "disciplinary division of labor" between those fields (Matsuda, "Composition"), this condition is obviously helpful for offering cross-cultural courses. At Penn State, as at many other colleges and universities, mainstream and multilingual composition are housed in separate departments. Aside from a lack of history supporting cross-cultural composition, there was also no ready mechanism for creating a single course staffed by both departments. My interest in piloting a course that would be sustainable meant that I felt the need to work within the disciplinary boundaries in place.

No advance advertising or "client" departments. I scheduled this pilot course as a regular composition section in order to perform the work of integration I have been advocating. As I have argued, the institutional history of second language writing—and of multicultural programs more generally—has operated following a logic of containment by which "diversity" options are sectioned off and labeled. Students often take these labeled courses as a way to check off diversity requirements for graduation (see Gilyard, *Let's Flip*), but the courses may offer little if any multicultural interaction outside of texts. In the specific case of composition, scholars have worried that L2-dedicated courses might segregate multilingual and monolingual users during their crucial first year (Matsuda and Silva). And others notice that students from diverse backgrounds are rarely encouraged to intermix academically or socially (Ibrahim and Penfield). So despite some concerns that failing to label an intercultural composition course as "special" would attract students who are not ready for this kind of work (Stärke-Meyerring), I did not advertise the course as intercultural or multicultural, nor did I seek connections between this course and other academic departments.

4. Unlike in Chapter 2, however, I discuss conceptual categories as they emerged during the course of the semester rather than devoting sections to discussing each category's emergence separately. I do this in an attempt to demonstrate students' developing awareness of their and their counterparts' linguistic and rhetorical strategies.

5. All excerpts from students' print and online compositions and comments are unedited.

6. There is a long tradition of English teaching in Saudi Arabia, much

of it coinciding with relationships between US oil companies and the Saudi royal family and related businesses. Sarah Benesch discusses the impact on English-language pedagogy of the need to train workers in oil fields.

7. Instead of tapping the university's standard online course management system, CyberLearning Labs' ANGEL, we asked students to post notes, drafts, and comments to a wiki hosted by a Penn State server. I had not found an easy way to merge the sites of two separate courses that were using ANGEL to allow them to share work across the courses easily. The wiki solved this problem because it allowed Susan, the students, and me to add content and even new pages and links to a site that did not limit students' use based on their course enrollment. To help students use the wiki, Susan and I scheduled a large computer lab for both classes. Students also used part of that class meeting to begin responding to group members' drafts.

8. After the first major assignment, the language-learning narrative, I did not require students to write major assignments on topics related to language. They were free to choose topics relevant to them and their prospective readers.

9. This omission has been made to avoid disclosing potentially identifying information about the student being quoted.

4

Composing Intercultural Relationships

> An intercultural rhetoric based on inquiry is, then, a deliberate meaning-making activity in which difference is not read as a problem but sought out as a resource for constructing more grounded and actionable understandings.
>
> —Linda Flower

> Successful "communication" is not judged solely in terms of the efficiency of information exchange. It is focused on establishing and maintaining relationships.
>
> —Michael Byram

THE DISCIPLINE OF COMPOSITION AROSE from institutional and national impulses to make tertiary-level education more efficient and to align that education with broad goals of cultural and linguistic purity and unity, especially in the face of rapid change. But approaching these goals has often come at the cost of nuanced understandings of cultural and linguistic diversity. Many teachers of composition (myself included) can recall productive class meetings, assignments, and even whole semesters spent writing and talking about the evolution of English as an international language, about experiences entering Discourses that often share boundaries with discrete languages and nation-states, about the powerful trope of "the border." But many of the same teachers (myself included) can also recall a point of diminishing returns, beyond which our attempts to bring these phenomena out of selected course readings and into the classroom itself—to take "diversity" seriously as a daily, lived experience and not just as a signifier for things going

on somewhere else—do not seem to make sense. In a ten- or fif-
teen- or even thirty-week course, organized by a logic of traditional
academic preparation and sorting, it is difficult for students and
teachers to justify what would surely be read as interesting, but
not ultimately practical, experiments with emerging linguistic and
rhetorical practices. No matter their putative content, composition
courses nearly everywhere are under pressure to produce writing
that translates quickly into US academic prose. And composition
teachers, pinned as they often are by their contingent statuses, have
little time to develop courses that would do something different.

Despite its contradictions and ancillary institutional position,
the uniquely American first-year composition course is remarkably
durable, and it is enough of a fixture in most colleges and universities that it can work as a springboard for ongoing critical language
work beyond a single course. But given the simultaneous complexity and practical necessity of reorienting ourselves to the multilingual realities of everyday communication, how can "comp" as a
truncated set of practices grow into *composition* as an opportunity
to design with ever increasing resources?

I have argued that the monolingual pedagogies of composition
are not only unethical but also impractical. And I have shown how
a pedagogical experiment both uncovered and started to implement
relevant attitudes and practices. However, pointing out a *need* to
change and describing an example of change do not easily lead to
a *program* for change. The suggestions I make, grounded as they
are in empirical and theoretical research and in my own teaching
and administrative experience, make neither composition teaching
nor administration—as they have developed up to now—more efficient. Instead, they require reviews of both theoretical perspective and daily interactions that can perhaps best be summarized as
a move from composition-as-writing to *composing relationships*. In
this move, it is important to note that writing is not outmoded but
rather put into circulation as an important communicative mode
that can sustain ongoing interactions. It is also important to note
that, while it could never give students enough time to *complete* an
education in composing intercultural relationships, the first-year
course is well positioned to play a key role.

TOWARD INTERCULTURAL COMPOSITION

As I started to explain in the previous chapter, composition can encompass a range of symbolic activities that include writing but that also expand well beyond it—especially if writing is primarily valued as an instrument of display and an opportunity for evaluation. As I related, Kenneth Burke may not have considered specific tertiary curricula when he wrote his own definition of *composition* (*Permanence*), but his articulation of how that term can reference a broad technology for addressing social uncertainty definitely opens a provocative question for compositionists: namely, is it possible to use the limited institutional ground that composition has in colleges and universities to undertake a potentially unlimited project of accounting for and leveraging myriad emerging competencies for intercultural communication?

The three fields that have had the most bearing on what I am calling intercultural composition—applied linguistics, rhetoric and composition, and second language writing—include instructors and programs that are frequently under pressure to ensure students meet conventional institutional marks for "competence." The necessary-but-ancillary position of first-year composition means that its teachers are often performing triage before sending student writers to "the disciplines." And second language writing courses are, as often as not, viewed as basic, precomposition, and even noncredit workshops. Constant Leung's comment about English language teaching in general seems applicable to this nexus of fields:

> The need to specify what is to be taught and learned inevitably turns research questions, which allow the possibility of both instability in existing knowledge and emergence of new knowledge, into pedagogic guidelines and principles which have to assume a degree of stability, transparency and certainty in existing knowledge. (125)

In Leung's view, then, translations from theoretical possibility to classroom solidity involve steep loss. But the makeup of the classrooms I have observed and taught in, the increasingly quotidian nature of students' multilingual and intercultural contacts, and uncertainties about exactly which language practices are worthwhile goals and standards all beg the question what kind of certainty pedagogic guidelines "have to assume."

"Certainty" with respect to successful language learning and use—whether oral, written, or technologically mediated combinations—applies less and less to discrete products and more to adaptive processes. Claire Kramsch and Anne Whiteside label this shift in criteria "symbolic" (rather than "communicative") competence. In a discussion that explicitly invokes *kairos* as a desirably nimble and tactical rhetorical technology, Kramsch and Whiteside define *symbolic competence* as one's "ability not only to approximate or appropriate for oneself someone else's language, but to shape the very context in which the language is learned and used" (664). They do not articulate specific teaching guidelines on the basis of this shift, but they do note that "symbolic competence is not yet another skill that language users need to master, nor is it a mere component of communicative competence. Rather, it is a mindset that can create 'relationships of possibility'" (667–68).

As dynamic as they can be, such relationships can still give educators a basis for developing pedagogic and programmatic guidelines. But establishing that basis requires looking a bit outside the typical nexus of fields that has informed intercultural composition in the United States so far. In what follows, I consider the utility of "intercultural communicative competence" as a guiding concept for teaching, assessing, and programming composition in inevitably multicultural and multilingual environments.

INTERCULTURAL COMMUNICATIVE COMPETENCE: SKILLS AND ATTITUDES

The idea of intercultural communicative competence (ICC) is a response to the Council of Europe's call to develop a Common European Framework of Reference for Languages: Learning, Teaching, Assessment (CEFR). CEFR is, in turn, a response to the Council of Europe's goal to "convert that diversity [of European languages] from a barrier to communication into a source of mutual enrichment and understanding" (*Common* 2). Given the European Union's twenty-three official languages and numerous other languages of influence, its ongoing need to manage the linguistic complexity of a large economic and political federation is apparent. Equally apparent are the overlapping histories of cultural and linguistic domination, evolution, and revolution on that continent—histories that have effects in languages now, in examples as diverse as Basque in France and Spain, Scots in the United Kingdom, and Hungarian in Slovakia. Within most EU countries, languages that can facilitate communication linguistically may present particular cultural challenges. My own experience in Poland was instructive. While Russian language signs were not uncommon in the eastern part of the country in the late 1990s, Poles who could translate the signs seemed fewer and farther between—despite the fact that many of them had been required to take Russian classes throughout primary and secondary school. They likely remembered enough to read the Russian, but the unloved legacy of compulsory language instruction within the Cold War Soviet sphere of influence made the memories uncomfortable.

The cultural baggage (welcome or unwelcome) that language inevitably carries is explicitly mentioned in principles set by the Council of Europe for language teaching: "languages" and "cultures" collocate in the first of these principles, and, in fact, the two make up a singular "valuable common resource." But the explicit mention of culture disappears from the following principle, which states that it is "only through a better knowledge of European modern *languages* that it will be possible to facilitate communication and interaction among Europeans of different mother tongues" (*Common* 2, emphasis added).

Intentional or not, the gap between teaching language and teaching culture gives ICC its project: to ensure that both linguistic and cultural elements of language learning are present from curricular planning through assessment. Language educator Michael Byram is perhaps most closely identified with articulating ICC as a pedagogical outcome. Through a series of books, Byram and his colleagues articulate theoretical bases for and course examples of intercultural language teaching. In doing so, they try to balance the messiness of cultural and language contact with the need to capture and systematize that messiness in teaching and administrative criteria. Byram begins to define this balance through metaphors of the sojourner and the tourist—figures that represent different travel experiences. The sojourner

> produces effects on a society which challenge its unquestioned and unconscious beliefs, behaviors, and meanings, and whose own beliefs, behaviors, and meanings are in turn challenged and expected to change. The tourist hopes for quite the opposite effect, first that what they have travelled to see will not change, for otherwise the journey would lose its purpose, and second that their own way of living will be enriched but not fundamentally changed by the experience of seeing others. (1)

For most people who choose to travel, the experience of being a tourist is the more common and comfortable one: travel ads may promote the dynamism of "foreign" cultures and people but usually against a backdrop of established—if not ancient—natural or monumental stability. Tour guides expertly conduct visitors through markets, around city centers, on rural safaris, all the while warning about gypsies and shady merchants, and policing other limits on intercultural contacts. For most people who are *compelled* to travel, owing to forced emigration, slavery, war, or other displacements, the sojourner experience is typical: there is rarely money, rarely a guide. Skills of cultural and linguistic adaptation are at a premium, as stories of slave songs and internment camp communication networks attest. Byram imagines language learners who, whether choosing intercultural contact or inevitably immersed in it, can effectively manage the relationship "between themselves and their own cultural beliefs, behaviors, and meanings . . . and those of their interlocutors" (12).

That ability to manage/to negotiate is the key component of intercultural communicative competence. While Byram's interest is ultimately in defining a criteria-based pedagogy that leads to measurable cultural and language learning outcomes, "competence" here requires a departure from many other methods of education, which are often in service of promoting group identity within institutions and countries. In the pedagogies that reductively operationalize the competencies Canale and Swain articulated, students are held to pretargeted linguistic and pragmatic standards: preferred codes (standardized/mainstream "English") and preferred modes and genres. Criteria for competence can thus be made clear. In ICC, however, replacing the (imagined) native speaker with an "intercultural speaker" puts criteria in play, since competence now

> includes the notion of discovery and negotiation but also adds the possibility that intercultural and native speakers—or intercultural speakers of different language and culture origins—need to negotiate their own modes of interaction, their own kinds of text, to accommodate the specific nature of intercultural communication. This might involve, for example, negotiated agreements on meta-commentary, on when and how to ensure that each interlocutor is able to interrupt the normal flow of interaction to ask for explanation of differences and dysfunctions, or to give a richer account of the presuppositions of a statement than would usually be necessary. (Byram 49)

These examples resemble the activities of composition students I have observed: that is, such negotiations, interruptions, and circumlocutions are already occurring not only in (foreign language) classrooms that are explicitly multilingual and intercultural, but also in classrooms in which linguistic and cultural contact might escape notice. Again, the question of prevalence should be a settled one. The challenge for pedagogies that rely on traditional assessments is that these interactions' high degree of complexity is not easily capturable. While there are certainly patterns—informed by culturally specific mores, immigrant experiences, and rhetorical preferences, to name a very few—cultural and linguistic contacts are by no means evenly distributed. Interlocutors' histories come into emergent contact with one another, necessitating the sort of "rhetorical listening" to which Krista Ratcliffe refers—a practice that requires co-rhetors to avoid the (relatively easy) extremes of assuming they are just like each other or that they are incommensurably different.

In view of these competing needs—to anticipate necessary communicative complexity *as well as* generate clear teaching criteria—Byram offers alternatives to the cross-cultural competencies that have long been a hallmark of the communicative approach to language teaching. He proposes five *savoirs*—a deliberate use of the French term because of its semantic range. *Savoir* connotes more than simply "knowing" a fact: as Byram reports learning from his French-speaking colleague, Genevieve Zarate, it encompasses intellectual and affective dimensions. But when paired with other verbs, it helps name the specific components of ICC:

> *savoirs*: knowledge of social groups, specifically of their internal practices and intergroup interactions
>
> *savoir être*: curiosity, willingness to learn from and adapt to interlocutors
>
> *savoir s'engager*: ability to identify—and make explicit—cultural values that affect intercultural relationships before they are created
>
> *savoir comprendre*: skills of interpreting and comparing documents and events from one's own and other cultures
>
> *savoir apprendre/faire*: ability to acquire new cultural knowledge and to adapt accordingly, especially in real time

Several *savoirs* can fit well into traditional assessment frameworks, which rely on students' making products that can be directly observed and evaluated. For instance, textbook and other received knowledge about foreign cultures and countries may be tested through traditional classroom exams and quizzes. Written and oral presentations are often useful media for assessing students' interpretations of documents. However, real-time/on-the-fly intercultural adaptation (*savoir apprendre/faire*) and attitudinal shifts about intercultural contact (*savoir être*) are much more challenging to capture. *Savoir faire*, for example, puts received cultural knowledge into play as communicators detect differences in the immediate and imminent circumstances of interaction; thus, interlocutors may be using a range of adaptive strategies that occur in places or at times not amenable to data collection or direct testing.

The Korean student who reported (in Chapter 2) on her fast negotiation of whether to use Korean or English told me what she
was thinking and doing after the fact—indirectly. Similarly, I was
aware in numerous classroom observations that my choice of one
mixed-language-background group over another meant that I was
choosing one set of interactions that I could partially capture over
another that I could not. *Savoir être* poses an even greater problem: how to assess attitudes. Byram suggests avoiding instruments
that ask students simply to express attitudes in favor of requiring
"action[s] demonstrating preference" (92). Students could, for example, choose among different media representations of a foreign
culture or country in the process of explaining it to someone else
who has never traveled there. Or they could integrate foreign perspectives on their own countries'/cultures' taken-for-granted beliefs
and actions. A dialogue potentially productive of such an outcome
was emerging between the student peer reviewers from the United States and the United Arab Emirates discussed in Chapter 3.
Ultimately, however, Byram projects that evidence for attitudinal
shifts will accumulate over time, and that a successful "intercultural
speaker" will produce such evidence in a portfolio, to be evaluated
along with more directly obtained data.

COMPOSITION CURRICULA AND
INTERCULTURAL DISCOVERY

As the Byram epigram that begins this chapter suggests, ICC anticipates that a significant part of learning other languages is learning about the emergent intercultural relationships that come about
through language contact. Often, successful interactions require
local appropriateness, which may trade off directly with linguistic
efficiency. This point is clear enough in the context of foreign language teaching: anyone who has gone from a grammar-translation-
based or audio-lingual or CLT-based foreign language course into a
target country learns quickly that communication involves significantly more than practicing textbook routines. Less clear, though,
may be ICC's application to "comp." Even though he articulates
ways to shift from native to intercultural competence criteria,

Byram in large part recapitulates applied linguistics' and foreign language teaching's focus on the speaker as the language learner: aside from discussing the importance of nonverbal communication and the role that documents play in interactions, Byram does not address writing. Additionally, Byram is explicit about focusing on *foreign* language learning contexts—those in which speakers of discretely different languages need to interact in recognizably multilingual and *multinational* spaces, such as the European Union. Indeed, Byram passes on taking up the issue of *second* language learning and teaching, owing to the complexities of applying principles of foreign language learning to multilingual and multicultural contexts within national borders. Of course, a hallmark of research on second language writing over at least the last decade has been the growing recognition of precisely such complexity: "second language" and "international" are by no means the same (Harklau, Losey, and Siegal; Roberge, Siegal, and Harklau). Nor are second language writers easily locatable solely within ESL-designated classes. So the national boundaries Byram imagines as he envisions ICC curricula cut across an increasing number of composition classrooms. And, by extension, the fieldwork abroad that he suggests for learners, which

> provides them with the opportunity to develop attitudes which include ability to cope with different stages of adaptation, engagement with unfamiliar conventions of behavior and interaction, and an interest in other cultures which is not that of the tourist or business person[,] can be had in those classrooms. (69)

Given the rich environments of many composition classrooms—environments shaped by the near-universal undergraduate writing requirement and by (sometimes hidden) cultural and linguistic complexity—cultivating ICC in composition seems not only a worthwhile goal but also a practically possible one. Granted, many composition curricula are already full of content that makes for extremely tight scheduling. However, the approach I advocate is not one that seeks to replace particular kinds of content with others. As

I hope I have made clear, shifting perspectives from composition as "comp" to composing intercultural relationships can and should happen where students, teachers, and administrators already are. So-called multicultural textbooks and courses sequester diversity-related content into clearly defined programs, courses, and/or instructional units within those courses. They also require students to read texts by diverse authors in identifiably "other" places. Intercultural composition in such settings becomes composing *about* other cultural experiences and rhetorics rather than composing *within* them, assuming they already pervade even the most apparently homogeneous spaces. So the specific pedagogical differences have more to do with method than with substituting certain assignments for others (Barro, Jordan, and Roberts). In general terms, this means courses that adopt an attitude of discovery and empirical groundedness similar to what I have modeled in this book. To be sure, there remains a place for more or less received understandings of topoi, organizational patterns, style, delivery schemes, and the influences of national cultures on all those considerations: this is Byram's *savoir*—the sort of knowledge about groups that comes, for instance, from contrastive rhetoric or from the durable five-paragraph theme. Both examples do provide key introductory information, but both also (productively) beg the question whether other options and other understandings are possible.

The suggestions I provide in the following sections for opening those possibilities and for capturing the work students produce are not intended to be comprehensive. Rather, they illustrate various ways that composition courses can infuse intercultural discovery and communication. But I also suggest that the composition pedagogies influenced by ICC do not merely require in-class or single-course adjustments. Discovery, adjustment to multilingual and intercultural contexts, and a focus on in situ or emergent communicative appropriateness clearly challenge programmatic and institutional assessment norms. In other words, while first-year courses—traditionally conceived and scheduled—may *initiate* pedagogies for composing intercultural relationships, they cannot bring such pedagogies to fruition by themselves. Therefore, my suggestions necessarily extend *beyond* "the" composition course as well.

Needs Analysis and Classroom Demographics

Even the most apparently homogeneous groups of students bring histories with them that are not easily or desirably checked at the door. It is impractical to assume that students who commonly speak or write in English among other languages, whose formal schooling was interrupted by voluntary or forced immigration, whose home-based literacy and orality differ from what they were explicitly taught, or who have been taught English language grammar by way of having their mistakes pointed out to them, will enter composition classrooms without presuppositions about their own and others' ability to compose. If a key goal of an intercultural composition course is not only to produce writing but also to animate writing as a technology for cultivating and sustaining relationships, then exploring such presuppositions is important. Various techniques for encouraging students to analyze and articulate their needs and their preclassroom attitudes about language use may be employed early in the course. In fact, the typical first-day writing warm-up or diagnostic essay, which often asks about prior writing courses or previous encounters with rhetoric, can be bolstered for such a purpose. Suggested topics relevant to plumbing students' contacts with and attitudes about difference include

- Previous linguistic misunderstandings (and attempts to repair them orally, in writing, or via other channels, such as texting)
- Culturally based misunderstandings, such as differences over gender roles or encounters with taboo subjects for conversation
- Arguments that were ultimately unresolvable because interlocutors lacked common ground
- Being corrected or correcting others
- Entering foreign countries and/or needing to use foreign languages
- Affective dimensions of everyday language contact, such as impatience in service situations
- Entering new discourse communities and being conscious of community-specific behaviors, expectations, and routines,

such as those in religious groups, on teams, on jobs, in extra-curricular societies, and in online forums

- Mismatches between textbook expectations and real situations, such as those between an employee manual and advice from actual employees

Instructors might also bolster other typical introductory tasks by asking students to provide information about themselves beyond what may appear on a class roster, such as native or first language(s). To be sure, however, students may be reticent about providing such information, especially in a stand-alone survey, for many of the same reasons they try to avoid labels such as "ESL": fear of stigma or of association and/or perceived irrelevance. Instead, instructors can encourage students to rethink and revisit the first-day topics as students consider what their specific course needs and goals are and as readings, discussions, and writing assignments during the course evolve. As I observed in the class I copiloted and in some of my observational research (especially with Cynthia, whose classes I discuss in Chapter 2), merely asking students to think about intercultural communication in composition is novel for many of them, and it can have heuristic effects beyond the single activity. Students who are reluctant to participate—especially in many US classrooms, where participation is synonymous with speaking during class sessions—may find more opportunities to contribute in those courses where instructors are up front about the ethical and practical dimensions of recognizing cultural and linguistic diversity *in class* as well as outside of it.

Specific Intercultural Assignments and Scaffolded Peer Interactions

Byram counterposes the "ladder" metaphor characterizing the linear, stepwise curricula of traditional language teaching (up to a native-language-user standard) to the "jigsaw puzzle" metaphor that concretizes his articulation of ICC. That is, where traditional curricula teach students up to a standard by way of a cumulative assignment sequence, ICC recognizes that at least some learning is not easily anticipated in advance curricular planning. As ICC's adaptive and attitudinal elements suggest, a language user's needs and resources will ultimately be grounded in interactions with other language users: in other words, Available Designs will vary depending on the situation. Certainly, ICC includes the concept of baseline knowledge of patterns of communication (previously Available Designs), but that knowledge is put into play by the exigent and emergent needs of communication (the process of Designing).

Assignments that both encourage students to reflect on and analyze cross-cultural and linguistic contact and negotiate that contact in real time are thus especially appropriate. Depending on results from early-course surveys and on curricular flexibility, instructors may feature explicitly intercultural content, requiring students to read and write about obviously multicultural topics. However, reading and writing *about* intercultural contact risks containing and distancing that contact from students where they are. In ICC terms, relying solely on this approach would risk perpetuating received knowledge (*savoirs*) without the necessary critical and productive element of adaptation *(savoir faire)*. James Paul Gee's discussion of Discourses provides a useful and accessible theoretical framework for composition students—one that describes tensions between relatively conservative forces of "culture" and "community" and evolving forces of cultural and linguistic contact in ways that mirror both the Design approach and ICC. The topos of "entering or adapting to Discourses" can prompt student discussion of and writing about adapting to new schools, new jobs, new memberships in social organizations. The topos might easily be the basis of an early-term writing assignment—a way to encourage students to think about their past literacy development (a longtime favorite composition assignment) but focus their attention and their writing on specific instances of Discourse negotiation. In an ethnically diverse basic writing course I taught some semesters ago, students responded to this sort of assignment by writing about the linguistic and other symbolic elements of joining varsity sports teams, choosing preprofessional majors, working in jobs in which they were in the minority as first-language English speakers, and entering the United States on student visas. While I would never suggest that the stakes of these negotiations are all substantively equal, I would suggest approaching such an assignment with an eye toward similarities in *methods* that students recall following as they sized up Discourses. While narratives about entirely different countries and language groups will certainly include descriptions of tentativeness, misunderstanding, and even failure, narratives about entering intracultural and national Discourses will, as well—and may usefully provide all students with examples of Discourse negotiation that does not have to appear exotic. With such a baseline of critical reflection on past experience, students can move into assignments that require them to do original research on communicative practices as they happen. For example, students might follow up a reflective assignment on past Discourse negotiations with an exploratory assignment requiring them to research the Discourse practices of a college or university community. Such an assignment would, in turn, require students to conduct the kinds of empirical research Byram suggests—research that usually receives only passing mention in many composition curricula.[1]

In-class peer review of these and other written assignments can provide many opportunities for on-the-fly adaptation. Of course, peer review has long been a staple of relatively de-centered, process-oriented composition classrooms—a practice entrenched enough that its role in most first-language courses is unquestioned. There is more debate about its effectiveness in second language and mixed-language-background courses, however. Soon after Vivian Zamel argued for the merits of the process approach in second language writing, practitioner-researchers began debating the specific application of peer review (Witbeck; Pack and Dillon). Arguments against its use point to possible intercultural conflict that could impair communication (Allaei and Connor), language proficiency issues that keep multilingual English users focused on technical correctness at the expense of larger-level discourse concerns (Nelson and Carson), and negative attitudes about peer versus teacher feedback (Zhang, "Reexamining," "Thoughts"), among other problems. Arguments in support include claims that peer review provides immediate audiences for multilingual students to try out rhetorical approaches (Mangelsdorf); that it helps with the development of English-language listening and speaking skills (Mittan); that it reduces social anxieties about language learning (Pappamihiel); and that it provides an important dry run for students' future professional interpersonal relationships (Belcher; Berg). Across the spectrum of opinions, though, is the consensus claim that peer review will definitely *not* be effective if it is not previously scaffolded. As unfamiliar with and resistant to peer review as mainstream US students often are, multilingual students may initially find it even stranger and less productive, often because students' perceptions of native-speaker primacy combine with their perceptions of near-unassailable teacher authority—a hallmark of many educational systems worldwide. Thus, even the term *peer review* is loaded for many students who encounter it, owing to its clear reference to peers' evaluating one another's work when they may not feel or seem qualified to do so.

In its place, I would substitute the term *scaffolded peer interaction* to suggest a wider scope for peer-to-peer work in intercultural composition. As I have noted, much current work on ICC foregrounds the figure of the "speaker," which poses problems for ICC's adoption as a relevant approach to composition pedagogy. But the peer interactions that are already so common across composition classrooms provide a clear entry point for (re)considering students' talk about rhetoric and writing. In addition to the language-learning benefits that, for instance, Robert Weissberg has documented, there are probable benefits for students' rhetorical work at various stages from invention through delivery and revision, some of which I observed personally. And those benefits are not unidirectional. Peer interactions can concretely model for students one of the guiding assumptions behind intercultural composition: that competence is not solely locatable in native speakers but instead may emerge as topoi and other elements of context call for pragmatic adjustments (also see House). Rather than acting as authorities on language issues, native-speaking students actually stand to learn quite a bit about rhetorical considerations from their multilingual peers. In a rare study of peer review among students with mixed-language backgrounds, Wei Zhu notes that multilingual students were equal to their monolingual native-speaking peers at making effective global comments about written drafts, relying on what Alastair Cumming refers to as "writing expertise" that preexists multilingual students' entry into English environments. Kate Mangelsdorf's observation about students' shifting perspectives as a result of peer review sessions in a second language context is particularly provocative for cross-cultural peer review because it confirms in a specific pedagogical context the claim from studies of English as a lingua franca that multilingual users bring substantial experience with negotiating cultural and discourse communities—a desirable skill for all students, regardless of language background. As I noted in the discussion of my piloted class, however, such ideas need to circulate in class early, and they should be normalized through the kinds of early writing assignments I have suggested and also through early interactions in mixed-background groups. Many instructors' plans to facilitate student conversations—about invention, responses to reading assignments, and early drafting in addition to final-stage "review"—are crucial in intercultural composition as a means to put linguistic and other rhetorical competencies into play.

Realia

Current, real-world multimedia is a staple of communicative foreign language education because it gives students clear evidence that their learning is closely connected to nonacademic contexts. It allows them to compare the often pedagogically sterilized version of the target language they hear and read in class with the messy and spontaneous version they would encounter where the language is spoken. Rhetoric teachers have used realia since at least the *progymnasmata* for various purposes from prompting imitation of effective strategies to introducing topics to showing evidence of accomplished writers' processes. In intercultural composition courses, realia could well serve both ends at once, maintaining a clear tension between static targets and inevitable flux.

Engrish.com is a website dedicated to cataloging examples of Japanese uses of English, especially in advertising. The site's (anonymous) webmaster claims to have lived and worked in Japan for ten years, learning Japanese to near fluency while there. His habit of collecting apparently problematic translations found an outlet on the World Wide Web in 1996, and his own contributions of engrish have steadily given way to more and more viewer-submitted examples, which range from store signs to soft drink bottles to anime and manga. The term *engrish* itself points to a well-documented similarity that native Japanese speakers of English hear between the phonemes /l/ and /r/—one that can prevent them from producing a clear distinction between those phonemes in speech. Thus, the term itself, and much of the webmaster's own commentary on his and readers' submissions, suggests error: in fact, in response to the FAQ "Why can't they get it right?," the webmaster responds that Japanese primary and secondary students routinely study English for up to a decade but that they "get little practical use since there are not enough native English speakers to practice with." However, immediately above that statement is another from the webmaster that lays out his view of engrish as a rhetorical tool:

> Most of the Engrish found on Engrish.com is not an attempt to communicate—English is used as a design element in Japanese products and advertising to give them a modern look and feel (or just to "look cool"). There is often no attempt to try to get it right, nor do the vast majority of the Japanese population (= consumers) ever attempt to read the English design element in question. . . . Quite often it is easier to come up with English names than Japanese for a particular product. New products are brought to the marketplace in Japan more than anywhere else in the world and Japanese words and slogans quickly get used up. Japanese graphic designers will often tell you that English is widespread because the Japanese writing script (or scripts) limits their creativity—there are only so many ways to display their language, and only so many different types of fonts to use.

What initially appears at engrish.com, then, is a collection of unintended jokes: clear Japanese misuses of English that reflect unsophisticated translation. But what emerges from examples and descriptions, such as the preceding one, is a much more complex picture: rather than being used to (attempt to) convey linguistic information, engrish is—arguably at least as often—used by rhetors more interested in borrowing characters and even typefaces to bolster their rhetorical resources. A link on the engrish.com FAQ turns the tables on these performances; viewers are directed to Hanzi Smatter (hanzismatter.blogspot.com), a blog that catalogs US-based appropriations of Chinese characters, especially in tattoos. While the focus on Hanzi Smatter is where tattooed Americans get the Chinese "wrong," that blog, along with engrish.com, exposes a gap between linguistic and other rhetorical uses of language.

That gap gives students of intercultural composition a rich example of language contact. Questions abound probing how students might make sense of that contact and of the compositions it gives rise to. What are students' affective responses to seeing engrish? Do certain uses provoke different responses? What patterns emerge within and across media and contexts? What possible next steps are there beyond initial confusion and misunderstanding? At what point is "error" *error*, and at what point does it suggest innovation?

In keeping with the discovery orientation at the heart of ICC, instructors might encourage students to treat engrish.com, Hanzi Smatter, and similar sites as corpora of emerging language use—growing collections of usage data that may yield to a variety of analyses. In the specific case of English, such corpora are sorely needed. Despite years of critical analysis of research programs and pedagogies that assume the primacy of native English varieties, comparatively little effort has been directed to building descriptions of English as it evolves by way of the hands and mouths of its users wherever they are. As Barbara Seidlhofer succinctly notes, "the language has spread, but its description has not" (202). Important efforts are being made, however. One example is VOICE, the Vienna-Oxford International Corpus of English, directed by Seidlhofer and headquartered at the University of Vienna. VOICE is a growing collection of mostly unscripted, face-to-face spoken interactions in English among interlocutors whose educational and social backgrounds are mostly in languages other than English. As of mid-2010, VOICE comprised approximately one million words from 1,250 speakers representing approximately fifty first-language backgrounds. Since registration with VOICE's website as well as noncommercial use of the data are free, instructors and students can study and compare transcribed examples of speech, observe and search for patterns, and adopt or adapt the corpus adminis-trators' descriptive categories (including interviews, question-and-answer sessions, and informal conversations) as guides for their own data collection and analysis. The utility of VOICE's focus on nonnative speakers of English as a lingua franca trades off with its exclusive focus on *spoken* uses, so students can also explore corpora such as the International Corpus of English (ICE), which com-bines spoken and written data from countries in which English is officially prominent. Whatever realia instructors employ, students should be encouraged to view their rhetorical work on English *as it evolves around them* as part of a more global effort to make sense of English's evolution.

Portfolios

ICC's focus on relationship building in intercultural contexts makes its pedagogy suitable for long-term projects, which might take students out of classrooms and even out of their home coun-tries. Beyond single study abroad opportunities that send groups of students to international destinations for short terms, and often among English-speaking peers, Byram advocates long-term separa-tion from home-country and home-language peers and instructors. Where students in many typical study abroad programs may amass "experience," Byram would have that experience become "learn-ing," by which, in this instance, he means "autonomous" abilities to recognize and adapt to new situations (69). In this regard, for-eign language curricula often have the advantage of longer contact with students beyond single courses: students in the United States major in foreign languages, but rarely in composition, writing, or rhetoric. So foreign language students may combine traditional course work with the more distant learning opportunities Byram suggests—all within established academic programs.

To the extent that composition is frequently a first-year gate-keeper program with one or two courses, extended student field-work with instructor follow-up is infeasible. However, instructors can build into their courses explicit requirements for students to take both a longer and broader view of intercultural composition than course constraints would seem to allow.

One point of built-in convergence between composition and ICC is a shared focus on portfolio-based assessment, which encourages students to take revision seriously, to document and reflect on their development, and to incorporate evidence of learning creatively. Many composition instructors and programs are already drawn to portfolios as a way to meet institutional and regional (and increasingly national) pressures to demonstrate outcomes while also meeting professional obligations to take seriously students' writing processes. In fact, the CCCC Position Statement on Writing Assessment (www.ncte.org/cccc/resources/positions/writingassessment) makes exactly this point in arguing for the value of portfolios over timed and/or machine-scored writing testing. And Byram sees a clear role for portfolios in assessing ICC, since several intercultural competencies cannot be observed directly in controlled or formal classroom settings. Instead, users themselves must reflect on and document their emerging abilities to anticipate and adapt to intercultural conditions. In addition, since users will likely encounter intercultural situations outside the bounds of class time and space, ICC portfolios often include materials that are not specific responses to class assignments, such as travel journals and multimedia documentation of travel experiences (107–8). In intercultural composition courses, portfolio assignments can be expanded to include direct and indirect (that is, student-reflective) evidence of adaptation through speaking, writing, and other media—that is, materials beyond drafts of individual assignments.

Portfolios can also include materials from outside the composition course: artifacts from (and reflections about) intercultural communication in other courses and outside school activities can encourage students to make connections between their everyday negotiations and critical in-class lessons on composing relationships.

Several students in the course I piloted, for instance, found cultural and linguistic difference where they did not expect it—in encounters with instructors in other high-stakes courses who were not readily understandable. While I cannot claim that their reflective work in my course made it easier for them to comprehend their international TAs, I do know that reflecting on their attempts to understand—and on their attitudes about understanding—significantly expanded their thinking beyond knee-jerk reactions to difference.

TIME TO COMPOSE

> At advanced graduate and professoriate levels, composition as a discipline engages in research on writing and, in that location, must depict the object of its research as an open system. At the same time, composition lives at the beginning levels of first-year composition courses largely by depicting its object—writing—as a closed system of known processes and practices that can be encapsulated in handbooks and rhetorics.
>
> —Rhonda C. Grego and Nancy S. Thompson

Grego and Thompson's succinct description of composition's dual identity also describes the exigence behind their studio-based approach to writing instruction—one that seeks to decouple writing support from remedial/basic/first-year-only courses. Composition in US colleges and universities has always been necessary but ancillary. Because it is necessary, it persists, despite cyclical arguments for its abolition. Because it is ancillary, it can be difficult to resolve the dilemma Grego and Thompson point out.

Composition is ultimately grounded in human relationships. Since relationships are inevitably complicated, communication always includes significant possibilities of misunderstanding—perhaps nowhere more apparently than in intercultural situations—even (especially) where interlocutors share a language with a putative standard. Depending on the power dynamics involved, such situations can easily become more than linguistic misunderstandings: frustration, suspicion, and even hostility are possible where speakers and writers of a locally dominant language (or language variety) encounter users of other languages or nondominant varieties. Several responses can result. One response is for different users to avoid contact altogether, which has never been practical. Globally, multilingualism is common—solid evidence that intercultural contact is a foregone conclusion. And even in parts of *this* country where homogeneity appears to be the rule, demographics are changing as quickly as communications technologies are making it easier and cheaper to chat across borders. Another response is to require users of other languages to learn the locally privileged standard—to emulate native users of that standard closely enough that potentially troubling differences are ironed out or obscured. But the implications of setting up a particular standard can be troubling. And the feasibility of training nonnative users to sound/write/act "native" is highly doubtful.

A third response requires time. It is conceivable, as David Crystal suggests, that English users will see the emergence of a world standard. It is just as conceivable, though, that Crystal's vision represents the enduring hope of a stable pedagogical target for English-language competence—that the rich description that would arise from such a project would convert to a relatively static list of directives. A more productive, pragmatic, and ethical project would involve keeping *both* research *and* teaching grounded in an imperative to discover how English linguistic and rhetorical practices are evolving through the hands and mouths of their diverse practitioners. Granted, planning curricula and courses and assignments around a moving target represents a significant challenge. The challenge becomes even more pronounced when the pedagogical suggestions I make in this chapter are carried beyond the typical first-year course, as they surely must be to ensure wide attention to the high stakes of multilingual contact. In specific terms of ongoing writing instruction, response, and assessment, it can be worthwhile for compositionists to think about how multilingualism can play a role in conversations with colleagues across the curriculum—especially perhaps in the sciences and engineering, which remain extremely attractive fields of study for international and multilingual students. Writing-across-the-curriculum support programs can help invested faculty members include assignments requiring preprofessional or disciplinary students to research rhetorical conventions across national boundaries. And much as compositionists should bring such a multilingual focus out of texts to where students are in their daily experiences on campus, colleagues in other parts of the university can require students to compose relationships—and corresponding intercultural skills—in work groups that mix language backgrounds and experiences. All of this work in and out of designated composition courses can then become part of students' undergraduate portfolios, which are increasingly popular among universities seeking to document whole-curriculum outcomes.

Owing to the situationally specific nature of multilingual and intercultural contact, however, it can be difficult to prescribe a pedagogical program. And I would resist such a move in any event for fear of limiting the heuristic value of the theoretical and empirical information I offer in this book to a closed-system approach to the teaching of writing. Perhaps the best way to think about this program to address multilingual realities, then, is to focus less on targets and more on method—and not just teaching methods, but research methodologies that, like the grounded approach I suggest and follow in this project, reinforce the role of discovery in multilingual interactions. This kind of grounding in classrooms can and should lead to learning that exceeds prescripted pedagogies. In foreign language courses, for instance, students' choice of one past tense instead of another is governed more often by sui generis factors present in immediate interactions than it is by lists of rules in textbooks—factors that users must methodically and continuously perceive as they interact. So, while learning those textbook rules may provide initial guidance to language users, the rules are ultimately in play as users adapt. In intercultural settings, the choice of one *language* over another may have less to do with a desire for technical correctness than with more affective considerations, such as group solidarity or "face." In short, rhetorical responses in and out of classrooms require far more complex judgments than those that can be listed and taught in a single course.

But composition can play a key role. A practice of composition that more fully inhabits the institutional space it has may provide a foundation richer than "academic writing." Indeed, the seeds are already present. For example, composition's entrenched articulation of writing processes—of attempting to produce "better writers, not better writing"—is much more than cliché. Teaching students that composition requires time to invent, to revise, to edit is teaching them that compositions are subject to evolving rhetorical conditions. The staple activity of peer review reinforces that idea, and sustained peer response in explicitly intercultural situations could reinforce it even more. The students I observed in regularly scheduled courses and those I taught in my pilot course were balancing writing-on-task with negotiating communicative uncertainties. They saw their individual (written) compositions in service of the (multimodal) relationships they were composing. As another example, many composition curricula teach students to think of their writing as ways to facilitate relationships between rhetorical "senders" and "receivers"—relationships that are one-sided so long as receivers are portrayed as passive consumers who should not have to work to understand. The widely critiqued but still circulating model of the "rhetorical situation," after all, shows sender/writer/speaker and receiver/reader/listener as equal partners. If true, the work of communicating is shared. And there are payoffs to be had in moving beyond frustrated or dismissive responses to the sender's perceived failure. I have documented several here: from linguistic innovations to disruptive nominations of challenging topics.

I am acutely aware of the workload that composition for multilingual realities represents not only for students but also for teachers. As critical as I am of pedagogical resources that reduce promising linguistic and rhetorical theories to lists, I fully understand that many composition instructors need to save time where and when they can. Composition instructors need more programmatic and administrative support as classrooms continue to diversify. College and university statements about the value of internationalization have become commonplace, but they all too often translate to increases in study abroad resources rather than resources for immigrant and international students in residence (Kubota and Abels).

Composition program directors can and should articulate their work as necessary not only to improving student writing but also to improving students' intercultural education. This is a rhetorical move intended to align composition with other units in interdisciplinary relationships, which can increase programs' visibility and potentially create larger targets for financial and other support. Many composition teachers feel unprepared to work with large multilingual populations in their courses—a feeling that may be partially remedied by cross-training with teachers in second language writing or linguistics programs or by exploring opportunities to team-teach. Tenure-line research faculty members and graduate students can investigate cultural and linguistic diversity among entering students as well as among students already in popular disciplines. They can also explore faculty expectations across curricula—research that can feed into the finer-grained needs analyses and surveys I have described.

Whatever the specifics, composition should be a research agenda, a pedagogy, and a practice that has discovery at its heart. The imperative to discover that I have described aligns well with many of composition's other, rhetorical, imperatives—chief among them to assess available means. The diverse English users populating composition courses have often had to find means wherever they could, engaging in an ongoing process of learning and use. Thus, they have much to teach.

NOTE

1. Two exceptions are Eleanor Kutz's *Exploring Literacy* and Bonnie Stone Sunstein and Elizabeth Chiseri-Strater's *FieldWorking*, both of which include numerous assignments designed to engage students in in-class and out-of-class empirical research projects.

WORKS CITED

Allaei, Sara Kurtz, and Ulla Maija Connor. "Exploring the Dynamics of Cross-Cultural Collaboration in Writing Classrooms." *Writing Instructor* 10.1 (1990): 19–28. Print.

Atkinson, Dwight, and Vai Ramanathan. "Cultures of Writing: An Ethnographic Comparison of L1 and L2 University Writing/Language Programs." *TESOL Quarterly* 29.3 (1995): 539–68. Print.

Bakhtin, Mikhail M. *Speech Genres and Other Late Essays.* Trans. Vern W. McGee. Ed. Caryl Emerson and Michael Holquist. Austin: U of Texas P, 1986. Print.

Barro, Ana, Shirley Jordan, and Celia Roberts. "Cultural Practice in Everyday Life: The Language Learner as Ethnographer." *Language Learning in Intercultural Perspective: Approaches through Drama and Ethnography.* Ed. Michael Byram and Michael Fleming. Cambridge, UK: Cambridge UP, 1998. 76–97. Print.

Barton, David, Mary Hamilton, and Roz Ivanič, eds. *Situated Literacies: Reading and Writing in Context.* London: Routledge, 2000. Print.

Bawarshi, Anis S. *Genre and the Invention of the Writer: Reconsidering the Place of Invention in Composition.* Logan: Utah State UP, 2003. Print.

Bazerman, Charles, and Paul A. Prior, eds. *What Writing Does and How It Does It: An Introduction to Analyzing Texts and Textual Practices.* Mahwah, NJ: Erlbaum, 2004. Print.

Bean, Janet. "Feminine Discourse in the University: The Writing Center Conference as a Site of Linguistic Resistance." *Feminist Empirical Research: Emerging Perspectives on Qualitative and Teacher Research.* Ed. Joanne Addison and Sharon James McGee. Portsmouth, NH: Boynton/Cook, 1999. 127–44. Print.

Bean, Janet, Maryann Cucchiara, Robert Eddy, Peter Elbow, Rhonda Grego, Rich Haswell, Patricia Irvine, Eileen Kennedy, Ellie Kutz, Al Lehner, and Paul Kei Matsuda. "Should We Invite Students to Write in Home Languages? Complicating the Yes/No Debate." *Composition Studies* 31.1 (2003): 25–42. Print.

Belcher, Diane D. "Nonnative Writing in a Corporate Setting." *Technical Writing Teacher* 18.2 (1991): 104–15. Print.

Benesch, Sarah. *Critical English for Academic Purposes: Theory, Politics, and Practice*. Mahwah, NJ: Erlbaum, 2001. Print.

Berg, E. Cathrine. "Preparing ESL Students for Peer Response." *TESOL Journal* 8.2 (1999): 20–25. Print.

Berkenkotter, Carol, and Thomas N. Huckin. *Genre Knowledge in Disciplinary Communication: Cognition, Culture, Power*. Hillsdale, NJ: Erlbaum, 1995. Print.

Berlin, James A. *Rhetoric and Reality: Writing Instruction in American Colleges, 1900–1985*. Carbondale: Southern Illinois UP, 1987. Print.

———. *Writing Instruction in Nineteenth-Century American Colleges*. Carbondale: Southern Illinois UP, 1984. Print.

Bialostosky, Don. "Bakhtin's 'Rough Draft': Toward a Philosophy of the Act, Ethics, and Composition Studies." *Rhetoric Review* 18.1 (1999): 6–25. Print.

Blackmore, Susan. *The Meme Machine*. New York: Oxford UP, 1999. Print.

Blanton, Linda Lonon, and Barbara Kroll, with Alister Cumming, Melinda Erickson, Ann M. Johns, Ilona Leki, Joy Reid, and Tony Silva. *ESL Composition Tales: Reflections on Teaching*. Ann Arbor: U of Michigan P, 2002. Print.

Bloom, Lynn Z., Donald A. Daiker, and Edward M. White, eds. *Composition Studies in the New Millennium: Rereading the Past, Rewriting the Future*. Carbondale: Southern Illinois UP, 2003. Print.

Boquet, Elizabeth. *Noise from the Writing Center*. Logan: Utah State UP, 2002. Print.

Braine, George, ed. *Non-native Educators in English Language Teaching*. Mahwah, NJ: Erlbaum, 1999. Print.

Brandt, Deborah. *Literacy in American Lives*. Cambridge, UK: Cambridge UP, 2001. Print.

Brereton, John C., ed. *The Origins of Composition Studies in the American College, 1875–1925: A Documentary History*. Pittsburgh: U of Pittsburgh P, 1995. Print.

Brodie, Richard. *Virus of the Mind: The New Science of the Meme*. Seattle, WA: Integral, 2004. Print.

Burke, Kenneth. *A Grammar of Motives*. Berkeley: U of California P, 1969. Print.

———. "Linguistic Approaches to Problems of Education." *Modern Philosophies and Education: The Fifty-Fourth Yearbook of the National Soci-*

ety for the Study of Education. Part 1. Ed. Nelson B. Henry. Chicago: U of Chicago P, 1955. 259–303. Print.

———. *Permanence and Change: An Anatomy of Purpose.* 3rd ed. Berkeley: U of California P, 1984. Print.

———. "Questions and Answers about the Pentad." *College Composition and Communication* 29.4 (1978): 330–35. Print.

Byram, Michael. *Teaching and Assessing Intercultural Communicative Competence.* Clevedon, UK: Multilingual Matters, 1997. Print.

Canagarajah, A. Suresh. "Interrogating the 'Native Speaker Fallacy': Non-Linguistic Roots, Non-Pedagogical Results." Braine 77–92.

———. "Lingua Franca English, Multilingual Communities, and Language Acquisition." *Modern Language Journal* 91 (2007): 923–39. Print.

———. "Multilingual Strategies of Negotiating English: From Conversation to Writing." *JAC* 29.1-2 (2009): 17–48. Print.

———. "Negotiating Ideologies through English: Strategies from the Periphery." *Ideology, Politics, and Language Policies: Focus on English.* Ed. Thomas Ricento. Amsterdam: Benjamins, 2000. 121–32. Print.

———. "The Place of World Englishes in Composition: Pluralization Continued." *College Composition and Communication* 57.4 (2006): 586–619. Print.

Canale, Michael. "From Communicative Competence to Communicative Language Pedagogy." *Language and Communication.* Ed. Jack C. Richards and Richard W. Schmidt. London: Longman, 1983. 2–27. Print.

Canale, Michael, and Merrill Swain. "Theoretical Bases of Communicative Approaches to Second Language Teaching and Testing." *Applied Linguistics* 1.1 (1980): 1–47. Print.

Carrington, Ildikó. "Tutoring International Graduate Students." *Writing Lab Newsletter* 27.4 (2002): 10–11. Print.

Carson, Joan. "Second Language Writing and Second Language Acquisition." *On Second Language Writing.* Ed. Tony Silva and Paul Kei Matsuda. Mahwah, NJ: Erlbaum, 2001. 191–200. Print.

Charmaz, Kathy. "Grounded Theory: Objectivist and Constructivist Methods." *Handbook of Qualitative Research.* 2nd ed. Ed. Norman K. Denzin and Yvonna S. Lincoln. Thousand Oaks, CA: Sage, 2000. 509–35. Print.

Chiang, Yuet-Sim D., and Mary Schmida. "Language Identity and Language Ownership: Linguistic Conflicts of First-Year University Writing Students." Harklau, Losey, and Siegal 81–96.

Chomsky, Noam. "A Review of B. F. Skinner's *Verbal Behavior.*" *Language* 35.1 (1959): 26–58. Web. 15 Mar. 2006.

Clarke, Adele E. *Situational Analysis: Grounded Theory After the Postmodern Turn.* Thousand Oaks, CA: Sage, 2005. Print.

Coe, Richard, Lorelei Lingard, and Tatiana Teslenko, eds. *The Rhetoric and Ideology of Genre: Strategies for Stability and Change.* Cresskill, NJ: Hampton, 2002. Print.

Common European Framework of Reference for Languages: Learning, Teaching, Assessment. Council of Europe, n.d. Web. 20 June 2010.

Conference on College Composition and Communication. *Students' Right to Their Own Language.* Spec. issue of *College Composition and Communication* 25.3 (1974): 1–32. Print.

Connor, Ulla. "Changing Currents in Contrastive Rhetoric: Implications for Teaching and Research." Kroll 218–41.

———. *Contrastive Rhetoric: Cross-Cultural Aspects of Second-Language Writing.* Cambridge, UK: Cambridge UP, 1996. Print.

———. "New Directions in Contrastive Rhetoric." *TESOL Quarterly* 36.4 (2002): 493–510. Print.

Connors, Robert J. *Composition-Rhetoric: Backgrounds, Theory, and Pedagogy.* Pittsburgh: U of Pittsburgh P, 1997. Print.

Cook, Vivian. "Competence and Multi-Competence." *Performance and Competence in Second Language Acquisition.* Ed. Gillian Brown, Kirsten Malmkjaer, and John Williams. Cambridge, UK: Cambridge UP, 1996. 57–69. Print.

———. "Going Beyond the Native Speaker in Language Teaching." *TESOL Quarterly* 33.2 (1999): 185–209. Print.

Cope, Bill, and Mary Kalantzis for the New London Group, eds. *Multiliteracies: Literacy Learning and the Design of Social Futures.* London: Routledge, 2000. Print.

Cope, Bill, and Mary Kalantzis, eds. *The Powers of Literacy: A Genre Approach to Teaching Writing.* Bristol, PA: Falmer, 1993. Print.

Crowley, Sharon. *Composition in the University: Historical and Polemical Essays.* Pittsburgh: U of Pittsburgh P, 1998. Print.

Crystal, David. *English as a Global Language.* 2nd ed. Cambridge, UK: Cambridge UP, 2003. Print.

Cumming, Alister. "Writing Expertise and Second-Language Proficiency." *Language Learning* 39.1 (1989): 81–141. Print.

Dawkins, Richard. *The Selfish Gene.* New York: Oxford UP, 1976. Print.

Delpit, Lisa. "The Silenced Dialogue: Power and Pedagogy in Teaching Other People's Children." *Harvard Educational Review* 58.3 (1988): 280–98. Print.

Delpit, Lisa, and Joanne Kilgore Dowdy, eds. *The Skin That We Speak: Thoughts on Language and Culture in the Classroom.* New York: New Press, 2002. Print.

Devitt, Amy J. *Writing Genres*. Carbondale: Southern Illinois UP, 2004. Print.

"Engrish FAQ." *engrish.com*. n.d. Web. 10 Aug. 2010.

Enoch, Jessica. "Becoming Symbol-Wise: Kenneth Burke's Pedagogy of Critical Reflection." *College Composition and Communication* 56.2 (2004): 272–96. Print.

Fairclough, Norman. *Discourse and Social Change*. Cambridge, UK: Polity, 1992. Print.

Ferris, Dana R., and John S. Hedgcock. *Teaching ESL Composition: Purpose, Process, and Practice*. 2nd ed. Mahwah, NJ: Erlbaum, 2005. Print.

Flower, Linda. "Talking across Difference: Intercultural Rhetoric and the Search for Situated Knowledge." *College Composition and Communication* 55.1 (2003): 38–68. Print.

Flowerdew, John. "Attitudes of Journal Editors to Nonnative Speaker Contributions." *TESOL Quarterly* 35.1 (2001): 121–50. Print.

Foss, Karen A., Sonja K. Foss, and Cindy L. Griffin. *Feminist Rhetorical Theories*. Thousand Oaks, CA: Sage, 1999. Print.

Freedman, Aviva, and Peter Medway, eds. *Genre and the New Rhetoric*. London: Taylor and Francis, 1994. Print.

Gee, James Paul. *Social Linguistics and Literacies: Ideology in Discourses*. Bristol, PA: Taylor and Francis, 1996. Print.

Gee, James Paul, Glynda Hull, and Colin Lankshear. *The New Work Order: Behind the Language of the New Capitalism*. Boulder, CO: Westview, 1996. Print.

Gibbons, Pauline. *Scaffolding Language, Scaffolding Learning: Teaching Second Language Learners in the Mainstream Classroom*. Portsmouth, NH: Heinemann, 2002. Print.

Gilyard, Keith. "Basic Writing, Cost Effectiveness, and Ideology." *Journal of Basic Writing* 19.1 (2000): 36–42. Print.

———. *Let's Flip the Script: An African American Discourse on Language, Literature, and Learning*. Detroit: Wayne State UP, 1996. Print.

Glaser, Barney G. *Basics of Grounded Theory Analysis: Emergence vs. Forcing*. Mill Valley, CA: Sociology Press, 1992. Print.

Glaser, Barney G., and Anselm L. Strauss. *The Discovery of Grounded Theory: Strategies for Qualitative Research*. Chicago: Aldine de Gruyter, 1967. Print.

Goldstein, Lynn. "Standard English: The Only Target for Nonnative Speakers of English?" *TESOL Quarterly* 21.3 (1987): 417–36. Print.

Graddol, David. *The Future of English? A Guide to Forecasting the Popularity of the English Language in the 21st Century*. London: British Council, 1997. Print.

Grego, Rhonda C., and Nancy S. Thompson. *Teaching/Writing in Third-spaces: The Studio Approach*. Carbondale: Southern Illinois UP, 2008.

Grimm, Nancy Maloney. *Good Intentions: Writing Center Work for Post-modern Times*. Portsmouth, NH: Boynton/Cook, 1999. Print.

Grobman, Laurie. "Rhetorizing the Contact Zone: Multicultural Texts in Writing Classrooms." *Reading Sites: Social Difference and Reader Response*. Ed. Patrocinio P. Schweickart and Elizabeth A. Flynn. New York: MLA, 2004. 256–85. Print.

Gumperz, John J., and Dell H. Hymes, eds. *Directions in Sociolinguistics: The Ethnography of Communication*. New York: Holt, 1972. Print.

Halasek, Kay. *A Pedagogy of Possibility: Bakhtinian Perspectives on Composition Studies*. Carbondale: Southern Illinois UP, 1999. Print.

Halliday, M. A. K., and Ruqaiya Hasan. *Language, Context, and Text: Aspects of Language in a Social-Semiotic Perspective*. 2nd ed. Oxford, UK: Oxford UP, 1989. Print.

Hansen, Jette G., and Jun Liu. "Guiding Principles for Effective Peer Response." *ELT Journal* 59.1 (2005): 31–38. Print.

Harklau, Linda. "From the 'Good Kids' to the 'Worst': Representations of English Language Learners across Educational Settings." *TESOL Quarterly* 34.1 (2000): 35–67. Print.

Harklau, Linda, Kay M. Losey, and Meryl Siegal, eds. *Generation 1.5 Meets College Composition: Issues in the Teaching of Writing to U.S.-Educated Learners of ESL*. Mahwah, NJ: Erlbaum, 1999. Print.

Harris, Muriel. "Cultural Conflicts in the Writing Center: Expectations and Assumptions of ESL Students." Severino, Guerra, and Butler 220–33.

Herrington, Anne, and Charles Moran, eds. *Genre across the Curriculum*. Logan: Utah State UP, 2005. Print.

Hinds, John. "Reader Versus Writer Responsibility: A New Typology." *Writing across Languages: Analysis of L2 Text*. Ed. Ulla Connor and Robert B. Kaplan. Reading, MA: Addison-Wesley, 1987. 141–52. Print.

Holbrook, Sue Ellen. "Women's Work: The Feminizing of Composition." *Rhetoric Review* 9.2 (1991): 201–29. Print.

hooks, bell. *Teaching to Transgress: Education as the Practice of Freedom*. New York: Routledge, 1994. Print.

Horner, Bruce, Min-Zhan Lu, Jacqueline Jones Royster, and John Trimbur. "Opinion: Language Difference in Writing: Toward a Translingual Approach." *College English* 73.3 (2011): 303–21. Print.

Horner, Bruce, and John Trimbur. "English Only and U.S. College Composition." *College Composition and Communication* 53.4 (2002): 594–630. Print.

Horowitz, Daniel. "Process, Not Product: Less Than Meets the Eye." *TESOL Quarterly* 20.1 (1986): 141–44. Print.

Houp, Wesley. "Bakhtin, Berthoff, and Bridge-Building: Tutoring ESL." *The Writing Lab Newsletter* 28.5-6 (2004): 11–12. Print.

House, Juliane. "Misunderstanding in Intercultural Communication: Interactions in English as a Lingua Franca and the Myth of Mutual Intelligibility." *Teaching and Learning English as a Global Language*. Ed. Claus Gnutzmann. Tübingen, Germany: Stauffenburg, 1999. 73–89.

Hymes, Dell. *Foundations in Sociolinguistics: An Ethnographic Approach*. Philadelphia: U of Pennsylvania P, 1974. Print.

———. "Models of the Interaction of Language and Social Life." *Directions in Sociolinguistics: The Ethnography of Communication*. Ed. John J. Gumperz and Dell Hymes. New York: Blackwell, 1986. 35–71. Print.

Hyon, Sunny. "Genre in Three Traditions: Implications for ESL." *TESOL Quarterly* 30.4 (1996): 693–722. Print.

Ibrahim, Awad El Karim M. "Becoming Black: Rap and Hip-Hop, Race, Gender, Identity, and the Politics of ESL Learning." *TESOL Quarterly* 33.3 (1999): 349–69. Print.

Ibrahim, Nizar, and Susan Penfield. "Dynamic Diversity: New Dimensions in Mixed Composition Classes." *ELT Journal* 59.3 (2005): 217–25. Print.

Institute of International Education. "International Students in the US." *Institute of International Education*. IIE, n.d. Web. 1 June 2010.

Ivanič, Roz. *Writing and Identity: The Discoursal Construction of Identity in Academic Writing*. Amsterdam: Benjamins, 1998. Print.

Jamieson, Sandra. "Composition Readers and the Construction of Identity." Severino, Guerra, and Butler 150–71.

Johns, Ann M. *Text, Role, and Context: Developing Academic Literacies*. Cambridge, UK: Cambridge UP, 1997. Print.

———. "Too Much on Our Plates: A Response to Terry Santos' 'Ideology in Compositions: L1 and ESL.'" *Journal of Second Language Writing* 2.1 (1993): 83–88. Print.

Johns, Ann M., and Tony Dudley-Evans. "English for Specific Purposes: International in Scope, Specific in Purpose." *TESOL Quarterly* 25.2 (1991): 297–314. Print.

Johnson, Donna M., and Duane H. Roen, eds. *Richness in Writing: Empowering ESL Students*. New York: Longman, 1989. Print.

Jordan, Jay. "Between and beyond the Covers: Local Cultural Questions and the Limits of Textbook Curricula." *CCC* 61.2 (2009): 390, W464–74. [*CCC* Special Symposium.] Print and Web.

———. "Rereading the Multicultural Reader: Toward More 'Infectious' Practices in Multicultural Composition." *College English* 68.2 (2005): 168–85. Print.

Kachru, Braj B. *The Other Tongue: English across Cultures*. 2nd ed. Urbana: U of Illinois P, 1992. Print.

Kaplan, Robert B. "Contrastive Rhetoric and Second Language Learning: Notes Toward a Theory of Contrastive Rhetoric." *Writing across Languages and Cultures: Issues in Contrastive Rhetoric*. Ed. Alan C. Purves. Newbury Park, CA: Sage, 1988. 275–304. Print.

———. "Cultural Thought Patterns in Inter-Cultural Education." *Language Learning* 16.1-2 (1966): 1–20. Print.

———. "What in the World is Contrastive Rhetoric?" Foreword. Panetta vii–xx.

Kapp, Rochelle, and Bongi Bangeni. "'I Was Just Never Used to this Argument Thing': Using a Genre Approach to Teach Academic Writing to ESL Students in the Humanities." Herrington and Moran 109–27.

Kaufer, David S., and Brian S. Butler. *Rhetoric and the Arts of Design*. Mahwah, NJ: Erlbaum, 1996. Print.

Kecskes, Istvan. "Formulaic Language in English Lingua Franca." *Explorations in Pragmatics: Linguistic, Cognitive, and Intercultural Aspects*. Ed. Istvan Kecskes and Laurence R. Horn. New York: Mouton de Gruyter, 2007. 191–218.

Kern, Richard. *Literacy and Language Teaching*. Oxford, UK: Oxford UP, 2000. Print.

———. "From Practice to Theory and Back Again." *Language, Culture, and Curriculum* 15.3 (2002): 196–209. Print.

Kramsch, Claire, and Wan Shun Eva Lam. "Textual Identities: The Importance of Being Non-Native." Braine 57–72.

Kramsch, Claire, and Anne Whiteside. "Language Ecology in Multilingual Settings: Towards a Theory of Symbolic Competence." *Applied Linguistics* 29.4 (2008): 645–71. Print.

Kroll, Barbara, ed. *Exploring the Dynamics of Second Language Writing*. Cambridge, UK: Cambridge UP, 2003. Print.

Kubota, Ryuko. "A Reevaluation of the Uniqueness of Japanese Written Discourse: Implications for Contrastive Rhetoric." *Written Communication* 14.4 (1997): 460–80. Print.

Kubota, Ryuko, and Kimberly Abels. "Improving Institutional ESL/EAP Support for International Students: Seeking the Promised Land." *The Politics of Second Language Writing: In Search of the Promised Land*. Ed. Paul Kei Matsuda, Christina Ortmeier-Hooper, and Xiaoye You. West Lafayette, IN: Parlor, 2006. 75–93. Print.

Kubota, Ryuko, and Al Lehner. "Toward Critical Contrastive Rhetoric." *Journal of Second Language Writing* 13.1 (2004): 7–27. Print.

Kutz, Eleanor. *Exploring Literacy: A Guide to Reading, Writing, and Research*. New York: Longman, 2003. Print.

Land, Robert E. Jr., and Catherine Whitley. "Evaluating Second Language Essays in Regular Composition Classes: Toward a Pluralistic U.S. Rhetoric." Johnson and Roen 284–94.

Lantolf, James P., and Steven L. Thorne. *Sociocultural Theory and the Genesis of Second Language Development*. Oxford, UK: Oxford UP, 2006. Print.

Lave, Jean, and Etienne Wenger. *Situated Learning: Legitimate Peripheral Participation*. Cambridge UK: Cambridge UP, 1991. Print.

Leki, Ilona. "A Challenge to Second Language Writing Professionals: Is Writing Overrated?" Kroll 315–31.

———. "Coping Strategies of ESL Students in Writing Tasks across the Curriculum." *TESOL Quarterly* 29.2 (1995): 235–60. Print.

———. "Cross-Talk: ESL Issues and Contrastive Rhetoric." Severino, Guerra, and Butler 234–44.

Lerner, Neal. "Punishment and Possibility: Representing Writing Centers, 1939–1970." *Composition Studies* 31.2 (2003): 53–72. Print.

Leung, Constant. "Convivial Communication: Recontextualizing Communicative Competence." *International Journal of Applied Linguistics* 15.2 (2005): 119–44. Print.

Leung, Constant, Roxy Harris, and Ben Rampton. "The Idealised Native Speaker, Reified Ethnicities, and Classroom Realities." *TESOL Quarterly* 31.3 (1997): 543–60. Print.

Lu, Min-Zhan. "Composition's Word Work: Deliberating How to Do Language." Bloom, Daiker, and White 193–207.

———. "An Essay on the Work of Composition: Composing English against the Order of Fast Capitalism." *College Composition and Communication* 56.1 (2004): 16–50. Print.

———. "Professing Multiculturalism: The Politics of Style in the Contact Zone." *CCC* 45.4 (1994): 442–58. Print.

Mangelsdorf, Kate. "Peer Reviews in the ESL Composition Classroom: What Do the Students Think?" *ELT Journal* 46.3 (1992): 274–84. Print.

Matsuda, Paul Kei. "Composition Studies and ESL Writing: A Disciplinary Division of Labor." *College Composition and Communication* 50.4 (1999): 699–721. Print.

———. "Contrastive Rhetoric in Context: A Dynamic Model of L2 Writing." *Journal of Second Language Writing* 6.1 (1997): 45–60. Print.

———. "The Myth of Linguistic Homogeneity in U.S. College Composition." *College English* 68.6 (2006): 637–51. Print.

———. "Second Language Writing in the Twentieth Century: A Situated Historical Perspective." Kroll 15–34.

Matsuda, Paul Kei, Michelle Cox, Jay Jordan, and Christina Ortmeier-Hooper. *Second-Language Writing in the Composition Classroom: A Critical Sourcebook*. Boston: Bedford/St. Martins, 2006. Print.

Matsuda, Paul Kei, and Tony Silva. "Cross-Cultural Composition: Mediated Integration of US and International Students." *Composition Studies* 27.1 (1999): 15–30. Print.

McCarthy, Keely. "Conversion, Identity, and the Indian Missionary." *Early American Literature* 36.3 (2001): 353–69. Print.

McKay, Sandra Lee. *Teaching English as an International Language: Rethinking Goals and Approaches*. Oxford, UK: Oxford UP, 2002. Print.

Medgyes, Péter. *The Non-Native Teacher*. London: Macmillan, 1994. Print.

Miller, Carolyn R. "Genre as Social Action." *Quarterly Journal of Speech* 70.2 (1984): 151–67. Print.

Mittan, Robert. "The Peer Review Process: Harnessing Students' Communicative Power." Johnson and Roen 207–19.

Murphy, James J., ed. *A Short History of Writing Instruction: From Ancient Greece to Modern America*. 2nd ed. Mahwah, NJ: Erlbaum, 2001. Print.

Nealon, Jeffrey T. "The Ethics of Dialogue: Bakhtin and Levinas." *College English* 59.2 (1997): 129–48. Print.

Neff, Joyce Magnotto. "Grounded Theory: A Critical Research Methodology." *Under Construction: Working at the Intersections of Composition Theory, Research, and Practice*. Ed. Christine Farris and Chris M. Anson. Logan: Utah State UP, 1998. 124–35. Print.

Nelson, Dana D. "'(I Speak like a Fool but I Am Constrained)': Samson Occom's *Short Narrative* and Economies of the Racial Self." *Early Native American Writing: New Critical Essays*. Ed. Helen Jaskoski. Cambridge, UK: Cambridge UP, 1996. 42–65. Print.

Nelson, Gayle L., and Joan G. Carson. "ESL Students' Perceptions of Effectiveness in Peer Response Groups." *Journal of Second Language Writing* 7.2 (1998): 113–31. Print.

Nelson, Marie Wilson. *At the Point of Need: Teaching Basic and ESL Writers*. Portsmouth, NH: Boynton/Cook, 1991. Print.

Newman, Beatrice Mendez. "Centering in the Borderlands: Lessons from Hispanic Student Writers." *Writing Center Journal* 23.2 (2003): 43–62. Print.

North, Stephen M. "The Idea of a Writing Center." *College English* 46.5 (1984): 433–46. Print.

Occom, Samson. "A Short Narrative of My Life." *The Elders Wrote: An Anthology of Early Prose by North American Indians, 1768–1931*. Ed. Bernd Peyer. Berlin: Reimer, 1982. 12–18. Print.

Ohmann, Richard. *English in America: A Radical View of the Profession*. Oxford, UK: Oxford UP, 1976. Print.

Pack, Alice C., and Deborah Dillon. "Peer-Tutoring Activities for the ESL Classroom." *TESOL Newsletter* 14.3 (1980): 10–11. Print.

Panetta, Clayann Gilliam. *Contrastive Rhetoric Revisited and Redefined*. Mahwah, NJ: Erlbaum, 2001. Print.

Pappamihiel, N. Eleni. "English as a Second Language Students and English Language Anxiety: Issues in the Mainstream Classroom." *Research in the Teaching of English* 36.3 (2002): 327–55. Print.

Pennington, Martha C. "The Impact of the Computer in Second Language Writing." Kroll 287–310.

Pennycook, Alastair. "Disinventing Standard English." *English Language and Linguistics* 4.1 (2000): 115–24. Print.

———. "The Myth of English as an International Language." *Literacy Learning: The Middle Years* 12.1 (2004): 26–32. Print.

———. "Vulgar Pragmatism, Critical Pragmatism, and EAP." *English for Specific Purposes* 16.4 (1997): 253–69. Print.

Pike, Kenneth L. *Language in Relation to a Unified Theory of the Structure of Human Behavior*. 2nd rev. ed. The Hague: Mouton, 1967. Print.

Pratt, Mary Louise. "Arts of the Contact Zone." *Profession 91*. Ed. Phyllis Franklin. New York: MLA, 1991. 33–40. Print.

Quandahl, Ellen. "'It's Essentially as Though This Were Killing Us': Kenneth Burke on Mortification and Pedagogy." *Rhetoric Society Quarterly* 27.1 (1997): 5–22. Print.

Raimes, Ann. "Out of the Woods: Emerging Traditions in the Teaching of Writing." *TESOL Quarterly* 25.3 (1991): 407–30. Print.

Rampton, Ben. *Crossing: Language and Ethnicity among Adolescents*. London: Longman, 1995. Print.

Ratcliffe, Krista. "Rhetorical Listening: A Trope for Interpretive Invention and a 'Code of Cross-Cultural Conduct.'" *College Composition and Communication* 51.2 (1999): 195–224. Print.

Reed, Carol E. "Adapting TESL Approaches to the Teaching of Written Standard English as a Second Dialect to Speakers of American Black English Vernacular." *TESOL Quarterly* 7.3 (1973): 289–307. Print.

Reid, Joy. "'Eye' Learners and 'Ear' Learners: Identifying the Language Needs of International Students and US Resident Writers." *Grammar in the Composition Classroom: Essays on Teaching ESL for College-Bound Students*. Ed. Joy Reid and Patricia Byrd. Boston: Heinle, 1998. 3–17. Print.

Reid, Joy, and Barbara Kroll. "Designing and Assessing Effective Classroom Writing Assignments for NES and ESL Students." *Journal of Second Language Writing* 4.1 (1995): 17–41. Print.

Richardson, Elaine. *African American Literacies*. New York: Routledge, 2003. Print.

Roberge, Mark, Meryl Siegal, and Linda Harklau, eds. *Generation 1.5 in College Composition: Teaching Academic Writing to U.S.-Educated Learners of ESL*. New York: Routledge, 2009. Print.

Savignon, Sandra J. *Communicative Competence: Theory and Classroom Practice: Texts and Contexts in Second Language Learning*. Reading, MA: Addison-Wesley, 1983. Print.

Schroeder, Chris, Helen Fox, and Patricia Bizzell. *AltDis: Alternative Discourses and the Academy*. Portsmouth, NH: Boynton/Cook Heinemann, 2002. Print.

Schuster, Charles I. "Mikhail Bakhtin as Rhetorical Theorist." *College English* 47.6 (1985): 594–607. Print.

Schutz, Aaron, and Anne Ruggles Gere. "Service Learning and English Studies: Rethinking 'Public' Service." *College English* 60.2 (1998): 129–49. Print.

Seidlhofer, Barbara. "*Habeas Corpus* and *Divide et Impera*: 'Global English' and Applied Linguistics." *Unity and Diversity in Language Use*. Ed. Kristyan Spelman Miller and Paul Thompson. New York: Continuum, 2001. 198–217. Print.

Severino, Carol, Juan C. Guerra, and Johnnella E. Butler, eds. *Writing in Multicultural Settings*. New York: MLA, 1997. Print.

Sifakis, Nicos C. "Teaching EIL—Teaching *International* or *Intercultural* English? What Teachers Should Know." *System* 32.2 (2004): 237–50. Print.

Silva, Tony. "Toward an Understanding of the Distinct Nature of L2 Writing: The ESL Research and its Implications." *TESOL Quarterly* 27.4 (1993): 657–77. Print.

Stärke-Meyerring, Doreen. "'Lost and Melted in the Pot': Multicultural Literacy in Predominately White Classrooms." *Outbursts in Academe: Multiculturalism and Other Sources of Conflict*. Ed. Kathleen Dixon. Portsmouth, NH: Boynton/Cook Heinemann, 1998. 135–57. Print.

Strauss, Anselm, and Juliet Corbin. *Basics of Qualitative Research: Techniques and Procedures for Developing Grounded Theory*. 2nd ed. Thousand Oaks, CA: Sage, 1998. Print.

Street, Brian V. *Social Literacies: Critical Approaches to Literacy in Development, Ethnography, and Education*. London: Longman, 1995. Print.

Sunstein, Bonnie Stone, and Elizabeth Chiseri-Strater. *FieldWorking: Reading and Writing Research*. 3rd ed. Boston: Bedford/St. Martin's, 2006. Print.

Swales, John M. *Genre Analysis: English in Academic and Research Settings*. Cambridge, UK: Cambridge UP, 1990. Print.

———. *Research Genres: Explorations and Applications*. Cambridge, UK: Cambridge UP, 2004. Print.

Thonus, Terese. "Serving Generation 1.5 Learners in the University Writing Center." *TESOL Journal* 12.1 (2003): 17–24. Print.

US Census Bureau. "New Census Bureau Report Analyzes Nation's Linguistic Diversity." U.S. Census Bureau, 27 Apr. 2010. Web. 1 June 2010.

Valdés, Guadalupe. "Bilingual Minorities and Language Issues in Writing: Toward Professionwide Responses to a New Challenge." *Written Communication* 9.1 (1992): 85–136. Print.

Weissberg, Robert. *Connecting Speaking and Writing in Second Language Writing Instruction*. Ann Arbor: U of Michigan P, 2006. Print.

Wenger, Etienne. *Communities of Practice: Learning, Meaning, and Identity*. Cambridge, UK: Cambridge UP, 1998. Print.

Widdowson, H. G. "The Ownership of English." *TESOL Quarterly* 28.2 (1994): 377–89. Print.

Williams, Jessica. "Tutoring and Revision: Second Language Writers in the Writing Center." *Journal of Second Language Writing* 13.3 (2004): 173–201. Print.

Williams, Jessica, and Carol Severino. "The Writing Center and Second Language Writers." *Journal of Second Language Writing* 13.3 (2004): 165–172. Print.

Wills, Tracy. "Tutoring ESL Students and Overcoming Frustration." *The Writing Lab Newsletter* 28.5-6 (2004): 8–10. Print.

Witbeck, Michael C. "Peer Correction Procedures for Intermediate and Advanced ESL Composition Lessons." *TESOL Quarterly* 10.3 (1976): 321–26. Print.

Wright, Elizabethada A., and S. Michael Halloran. "From Rhetoric to Composition: The Teaching of Writing in America to 1900." Murphy 213–46.

Zamel, Vivian. "Teaching Composition in the ESL Classroom: What We Can Learn from Research in the Teaching of English." *TESOL Quarterly* 10.1 (1976): 67–76. Print.

Zhang, Shuqiang. "Reexamining the Affective Advantage of Peer Feedback in the ESL Writing Class." *Journal of Second Language Writing* 4.3

(1995): 209–22. Print.

———. "Thoughts on Some Recent Evidence Concerning the Affective Advantage of Peer Feedback." *Journal of Second Language Writing* 8.3 (1999): 321–26. Print.

Zhu, Wei. "Interaction and Feedback in Mixed Peer Response Groups." *Journal of Second Language Writing* 10.4 (2001): 251–76. Print.

INDEX

AUTHOR

Jay Jordan is assistant professor in the Department of English and the University Writing Program at the University of Utah, where he also coordinates the university's required, lower-division writing course. He is author or coauthor of articles and edited collections on multilingualism in composition pedagogy and theory. He serves as cochair of the CCCC Committee on Second Language Writing.

OTHER BOOKS IN THE CCCC STUDIES IN WRITING & RHETORIC SERIES

Redesigning Composition for Multilingual Realities
Jay Jordan

Agency in the Age of Peer Production
Quentin D. Vieregge, Kyle D. Stedman, Taylor Joy Mitchell, and Joseph M. Moxley

Remixing Composition: A History of Multimodal Writing Pedagogy
Jason Palmeri

First Semester: Graduate Students, Teaching Writing, and the Challenge of Middle Ground
Jessica Restaino

Agents of Integration: Understanding Transfer as a Rhetorical Act
Rebecca S. Nowacek

Digital Griots: African American Rhetoric in a Multimedia Age
Adam J. Banks

The Managerial Unconscious in the History of Composition Studies
Donna Strickland

Everyday Genres: Writing Assignments across the Disciplines
Mary Soliday

The Community College Writer: Exceeding Expectations
Howard Tinberg and Jean-Paul Nadeau

A Taste for Language: Literacy, Class, and English Studies
James Ray Watkins

Before Shaughnessy: Basic Writing at Yale and Harvard, 1920–1960
Kelly Ritter

Writer's Block: The Cognitive Dimension
Mike Rose

Teaching/Writing in Thirdspaces: The Studio Approach
Rhonda C. Grego and Nancy S. Thompson

Rural Literacies
Kim Donehower, Charlotte Hogg, and Eileen E. Schell

Writing with Authority: Students' Roles as Writers in Cross-National Perspective
David Foster

Whistlin' and Crowin' Women of Appalachia: Literacy Practices since College
Katherine Kelleher Sohn

Sexuality and the Politics of Ethos in the Writing Classroom
Zan Meyer Gonçalves

African American Literacies Unleashed: Vernacular English and the Composition Classroom
Arnetha F. Ball and Ted Lardner

Revisionary Rhetoric, Feminist Pedagogy, and Multigenre Texts
Julie Jung

Archives of Instruction: Nineteenth-Century Rhetorics, Readers, and Composition Books in the United States
Jean Ferguson Carr, Stephen L. Carr, and Lucille M. Schultz

Response to Reform: Composition and the Professionalization of Teaching
Margaret J. Marshall

Multiliteracies for a Digital Age
Stuart A. Selber

This book was typeset in Garamond and Frutiger by Barbara Frazier.
Typefaces used on the cover include Adobe Garamond and Formata.
The book was printed on 55-lb. Natural Offset paper
by Victor Graphics, Inc.